PLEASE DON'T TAKE ME HOME:

A CAT CALLED ROBSON-KANU

ANDREW FOLEY JONES

Please Don't Take Me Home
A Cat Called Robson-Kanu

By Andrew Foley Jones

Please Don't Take Me Home - A Cat Called Robson-Kanu. This book was first published in Great Britain in paperback during December 2016.

The moral right of Andrew Foley Jones is to be identified as the author of this work and has been asserted by him in accordance with the Copyright, Designs and Patents Act of 1988.

All rights are reserved and no part of this book may be produced or utilized in any format, or by any means, electronic or mechanical, including photocopying, recording or by any information storage or retrieval system, without prior permission in writing from the publishers – Coast & Country/Ads2life. ads2life@btinternet.com

A portion of this work was previously published in the Daily Post in 2016 and in Cultured Vulture in 2015.

This is a work of fiction. Names, characters, places and incidents either are a product of the author's imagination or are used fictitiously and any resemblance to actual persons, living or dead, events, or locals is entirely coincidental.

All rights reserved.

ISBN-13: 978-1540581037

Copyright © December 2016 Andrew Foley Jones

PLEASE DON'T TAKE ME HOME: A CAT CALLED ROBSON-KANU

What I am about to write, really did happen.

I have changed the identities of some of the protagonists to preserve their privacy.

Those of you who were involved, will, perhaps recognise yourselves.

And to the man who said we're just a peninsula on the edge of England, I hope you enjoyed your summer.

ABOUT ANDREW FOLEY JONES

St Asaph born Andrew Foley Jones was raised in the North Wales coastal town of Prestatyn and has since, whilst living in various areas of the U.K. retained a strong feeling of Welshness, still holding a season ticket for his beloved Wrexham FC, crossing the border from Chester where he now lives, rarely missing a home game.

A columnist for magazine and newspaper, he had his first work of fiction, 'Seductive Amoebae' published in 2008, followed by the cryptically titled 'Starbucks Ate My Lobster' in 2013 and 'The Laws Of Bigamy Do Not Apply To Daleks.'

His books have sold far and wide and received rave reviews with his often unusual and controversial style and whilst football is often referenced in his works of fiction this is the first time he has created a book with football at its very heart.

In his recent Daily Post column, he summed up what it means to support a football team: ""*Football is in the blood, in our soul. It is part of our lives, it can determine, often subliminally our mood, our productivity. It's a major part of our DNA, it's part of what makes us what we are.*"

ALSO BY ANDREW FOLEY JONES:

SEDUCTIVE AMOEBAE

STARBUCKS ATE MY LOBSTER

THE LAWS OF BIGAMY DO NOT APPLY TO DALEKS

CONTACT

WEBSITE: www.andrewfoleyjones.com

TWITTER: @Afoleyjones

FACEBOOK: Andrew Foley Jones

WALES: A FEW FACTS

Wales is a country in southwest Great Britain known for its rugged coastline, mountainous national parks, distinctive Welsh language and Celtic culture. Cardiff, the capital, is a refined coastal city with a nightlife scene and a medieval castle with ornate Gothic Revival interiors. In the northwest, Snowdonia National Park has lakes, glacial landforms, hiking trails and a railway up to the peak of Snowdon.

Capital: Cardiff

Area: 20,761 km²

Population: 3.063 million (2011)

National anthem: Hen Wlad Fy Nhadau

THANKS

To everybody who shared our wonderful summer and especially to Richard, Don Hale, Steve Green, my family, SFJ and baby bump.

Picture of the Wales crest on my top (taken by unknown German photographer).

Please Don't Take Me Home - A Cat Called Robson-Kanu

INTRODUCTION

I'm writing this at the end looking back, I suppose, like most things, with a tinge of colour from memory, thoughts that have been processed in a photographers lab in a basement somewhere, in the time since it all took place; a journey of sorts - a wonderful colourful journey of enlightenment and simple adventure.

I'm writing this from India, a district called Kerala in the south, known locally as "Gods Own Country" a place my dad always referred to as Prestatyn, my home town, as you drive down the hill from Gwaenysgor and the Vale of Clwyd flattens out beneath you, rising in the distance for the mountains of Snowdonia, the Great Orme of Llandudno, stretching into the Irish Sea like a tail of a great Welsh dragon.

My dad can never understand the need to travel to faraway remote places when there are better alternatives all within a two hour drive of his Prestatyn Home. I'm Face Timing him and my mum from a cliff looking over a beautiful Indian beach. He loves Face Time – it means he doesn't have to come and visit, we can have a chat, he can mock my bad beard and he doesn't have to leave the confines of his wonderful town.

"What do you think to this?" I say, turning the camera around to watch the dramatic swell crashing onto a pristine beach, the pretty colourful fishing boats drifting beneath the horizon towards the nearby Port of Kovalam. It's absolutely beautiful. I've been to India a few times and it always takes away my breath.

"No better than Rhosneigr" is his genuine heart felt response.

"Besides, if I want to see an Indian sunset, I can go to U Tube or Google Earth and then, there's that great documentary by Rick Stein: you can cook a great curry from that."

"And all from the comfort of your own sofa" I mimic.

"Exactly" he responds.

"Bucket lists, they're for losers" he adds, probably correctly.

Don't get me wrong, it's not that he nor my mother have not led colourful lives, they most certainly have; they've just perhaps reached a stage where they know what they like and all that: to be so contented is a great trait. I give you that father.

I've just finished my inaugural session of Yoga on a platform that overlooks a feisty grey sea that blasts its frothy white hands onto the sand reaching for the shore, the canopy of jungle that spreads in every direction in shades of every form of green and yellow. It's a stunning location, whatever your beliefs.

I've never done Yoga before. I've never even considered Yoga before. Apart from football, I'm not a big fan of group participation. I feel self conscious, clumsy, as awkward as a one legged man in an arse kicking competition. I'm as coordinated as a bowl of jelly – you get the picture.

I once, went to a step aerobics class (don't ask) and if back then, there had been mobile phones with video facility I would have become a U Tube Sensation. Honestly - it was that comical, I could see that at the time - all these women in fluorescent Lycra, many with those leg warmers they used to wear in the eighties despite it being a scorcher, were literally wetting themselves as I somehow defied gravity and performed routines that simply weren't suitable for the human form.

Anyhow, my long suffering partner, who I should at this point, introduce to proceedings, Sarah, who will be known as SFJ, suggested I try it 'just the once' to see if it assists amongst other things, with my woeful sleep, my woeful coordination and my woeful farts.

So I confess, it is with a sense of utter, unadulterated trepidation that I approach the achingly beautiful platform where the hotel has advised, Yoga sessions take place daily at 7am. I am very nervous, pathetic as it may seem.

I stand in my t shirt and shorts and watch this small man, dressed in what looks like orange martial arts attire and who must be in his nineties, I joke not. He looks like he should be in one of those spoof movies Leslie Nielsen always appeared in, like Aeroplane or an equivalent for Yoga teachers; it's as if it's how we would perceive a stereotype Yoga teacher to look like. But I really shouldn't mock, for it soon transpires, he is the Real Deal, don't you worry about that.

We begin by sitting cross legged staring out towards the Arabian Sea. He urges us to close our eyes and hold our hands open to the heavens. He tells us to breathe in and then out and does this over and over making noises as he instructs. I let out a fart, inadvertently and a man from Bratislava wearing his national's national kit eyes me with what I perceive to be disgust. It smells of the fish curry I had for breakfast. I knew I should have gone for the bacon sandwich.

He says in really rubbish English: "Body is the greatest doctor, food is the greatest medicine remember that. Respect your body: too many people fill it with poison."

I swear he's looking at me, my clenched buttocks probably causing me to be pulling a face like one of those gurners you often used to see in competitions in Barnsley or Doncaster. I'm really not enjoying this.

I'm still breathing in and out, trying to think of nothing, like he tells us, just allowing the energies that work within us with Yoga literally meaning "uniting together." Anyhow, you can do your own research if you are so presupposed. It really isn't very easy.

Nevertheless, there's something almost out of this body, sitting here, the wind blowing across me, the sound of the sea and the morning chorus of birds and insects coming to life. It's almost spiritual. I feel like I'm floating. I wonder how Wrexham are getting on – must be half time by now.

The Yogi (seriously known as The Bear by the locals, I joke note) in badly punctuated English points at my t shirt that, besides an cheap chronographic image of Joe Allen, adorns adjacent to it the words: 'The Welsh Pirlo' and asks "who is this" shaking his head unnaturally fast like a spoof Indian in a 1970s sitcom or part of a Donald Trump Lecture of The Danger Of Immigration In The New Millennium.

I laugh and notice beyond him, a sea eagle arcing through a pavement coloured sky, falling now towards the sea, out of view behind a sandstone rock, emerging seconds later, a large droopy fish, probably mahi mahi, dangling from its yellow beak.

He points again, his unimaginably clear green eyes, looking towards the image on my t shirt.

"Who is this?" he asks again, his head shaking like a snow globe.

I look down, glancing over the contents of the dark red jersey, that ripples across my torso in the early morning sea breeze, the left nostril of Joe Allen, hanging somehow ceremoniously from my right nipple.

"Aw this" I say, subliminally awkward perhaps at the apparent inappropriate attire for the surroundings: a football related garment in such a place of overwhelming spiritual beauty.

"This" I say, pointing to Joe's gently stumbled features, a languid smile on his industrious face.

"This" I say, like I'm introducing a rarely visited uncle at a wedding of a cousin to a new girlfriend.

"This, Mr Yogi," (yes, seriously call him, can you believe it, Mr

Yogi) "this is the wonderful, midfield Dynamo, Joe Allen, or as we like to call him, the Welsh Pirlo."

He looks up and down my chest; if I were a woman, he would be viewed as a rather lecherous administrator of Yoga and possibly stuck off or sent off for penance in some monastery on the slopes of a distant rarely visited mountain where they don't have wi fi, Sky Sports or Yoga Monthly.

"Ah, Wales" he remarkably comes out with, grabbing me by my overstretched shoulder blades, dancing me absurdly around the Yoga platform, singing as he throws me towards the floor, the lyrics "hey big spender, spend a little time with me" - I love Shirley Bassey; she's my most favourite singer, obviously of all time."

He pulls me up; the sea eagle swoops again towards the crashing waves looking for his next course.

"I love the Wales. Beautiful country. And I mean, to get to the semi finals with what, a population of what, 3 million people? And there's your England, I don't like the England, with their overpaid players - what his name, the man with the funny hair, plays for Manchester, and that man who play for who is it, the Liverpool, they have no hunger, no desire, they too rich and too stupid. They don't care if they win or no. You understand?"

I nod, the sea eagle drifts across the sky, his wings perfectly still, unmoving, just being propelled by the ebbs and flows of the wind.

"The Wales, they different, they play with a passion, a strength, they proud of their history, their heritage, they want to do good for their people. Wales and Iceland, I like these teams, I like these people."

He strokes the face of Joe Allen and with it, inadvertently I think, enters my belly button, sending a cold shrill through my body and says:-

"You think I don't know who this man is; this is not the third world you know – this is Joe Allen, he is my most favourite footballer in the entire world."

This is unreal. Here I am doing Yoga with a man who knows stuff about Welsh football; It's pretty weird. He's apparently some kind of Guru in these parts – people travel hundreds of miles to have an audience with him.

"I truly believe you can make the World Cup, I really do. I mean, Austria flopped at the finals, Ireland are Ireland, Moldova aren't up too much and Serbia and Georgia, whilst both, admittedly difficult obviously away from home, I think the group is there for the taking. You just need to keep your heads" he says, gesturing with both his index fingers to the edge of his temples in the internationally acknowledged sign language adopted by managers and football coaches world wide, signifying the need to 'keep it safe for 5 minutes - you know it's statistically the most dangerous time to concede when you've just scored a goal.'

He then performs an act that I wasn't expecting to see: he drifts away, perhaps ten metres from where I'm standing and controls an imaginary ball that seemingly drifts towards him through the morning Indian sky, traps it, ignores the run of Neil Taylor, looking away from goal, on his right hand side, and silhouettes, the imaginary Belgian defence, sent deep into the grey froth of the Arabian Sea, turning fully now, sending an imaginary shot powerfully, emphatically into the imaginary net.

He then turns away, reeling like the sea eagle, and runs towards the imaginary bench, cheekily ignoring it for a moment, before throwing himself on the collective human blanket that Messrs Coleman and squad provided in that moment of sheer unbridled joy that took place on a euphoric summer night on the French/Belgian border.

Myself and the Yogi embrace with all the verve and emotion that three million Welsh may have done at that wonderful moment. I remember the truly wondrous commentary that I've listened to since, over and over, on the television coverage, the amazingly atmospheric medium of a radio broadcast that always somehow seems somehow more magical. Even Robbie Savage's Wrexham twang captured the iconic moment with a certain beauty that will forever remain with me.

It's far from being a typical day. It's not yet 7am. I've done an hours Yoga in a remote part of India and I'm chatting all things Welsh football with a ninety year old Yogi. It's as a professional footballer who still appears to be without a job a few weeks into the new season might remark '... been a pretty surreal few weeks."

Please Don't Take Me Home - A Cat Called Robson-Kanu

That night, I watch the Wrexham York game unfold on the live thread of the Wrexham FC fans forum known as Red Passion. I like to watch it in ten minute lumps. We're one nil up, then it's one all and then not much appears to be happening and I'm trying not to give two shits but I know really deep down I do and despite us being in the fifth tier of English football, it still hurts the same, it still fills your being with euphoria when you win – it's completely irrational. I'm a grown man. I know it's irrational but still, I sit here, wasting time watching an I Pad screen, refreshing the page over and over, willing a goal, sitting here in my lucky underpants that must surely be the unluckiest lucky underpants ever to have existed. Still, these things we do, wear, the customs we think, just, might have a bearing on a game, on a result. It's truly baffling.

Football is in the blood, in our soul. It is part of our lives, it can determine, often subliminally our mood, our productivity. It's a major part of our DNA, it's part of what makes us what we are.

I'm eating a jackfruit that are all the rage over here – massive things that grow in trees and often fall and land on the heads of passers by, killing more people each year than sharks is, a waiter told me, a statistical truth: the things you learn when travelling.

Amazingly we snatch a seemingly unconvincing two one victory and my mood is instantly enhanced. I am a fickle soul. Red Passion becomes its typical hotbed of debate: the frothers or doom and gloom merchants versus the optimists or the happy clappers. Without getting all GCSE Sociology on you, it really is a fascinating microcosm of social structure; a Petri dish if you like, of how a society is made up.

The Happy Clappers are telling the world to celebrate the three points, enjoy the moment of pleasure that victory brings. On the other side of the debate, people are saying "wake up and smell the coffee" and "is this the level we've now accustomed ourselves too."

I love reading it. I used to contribute regularly but rarely do now. I might start again soon. Respect to everyone who does as it really is the heart beat of the club, whichever way you look at it. Without such passion, clubs like Wrexham would simple cease to exist, and remember, we really nearly didn't. So next time you want to chin someone who holds a differing view, count to ten, turn your palms skywards and mutter 'RELEASE.' Remember, it's better to care than to not give a shit – it's the apathy after all that will kill us.

Thinking of this convinces me to finish off the journal of my trip to France in the summer of 2016; it encourages me to bring together the anecdotes, the memories, the emotions, a diary of sorts of a summer that after years of defeat and disappointment, I never thought I would experience in my lifetime.

So this is the creation of such thoughts: ultimately a book after football but I suppose, there's some stuff there that is also about life and faith and existence and the way the world is forever changing; and without getting too spiritual about it, it's sometimes good to go something different, as my good friend Jonathon Rogers always says, put yourself out of your comfort zone.

So feeling rather upbeat about the decision to write this book, I've been persuaded by SFJ to have a session with the doctor to see if she can help with my sleep problems. You see, I really don't sleep much. Not sure what you have to do to be classed an insomniac but I must be close to it - if you can help me get some decent shut eye doctor, that would be just great.

She talks to me with a clip board and beyond her, all jangling chimes and statues of Ganesh the Hindu Elephant God sit around everywhere. There's a smell of ginger and cinnamon and other spices and she pours me green tea, spooning honey into the liquid mixing it with a spoon that sure enough, has the image of Ganesh at the top of its handle.

I go through to a room where more wind chimes dangle and then there's a natural wind blowing across my body, whale noises in the background and the hands of a man pouring hot oil onto my back.

As he kneads across my shoulder blades, my backbone and down across my tight hamstrings, I wince and then attempt to suppress laughter as he tickles my feet and then pulls each toe, the tendons clicking with each action.

He turns me over and it's difficult not to feel incredibly self conscious lying front end up naked, covered in oil wearing a thong Jordan or David Beckham would be proud of. And despite the gorgeous setting and the goodness that this is undoubtedly creating both physically and mentally, I can't help but fear either of two things: inadvertent flatulence or worse still, an unintentional erection.

A stray fart with hindsight could be nothing much: the spicy food and the massaging motion on places of the body not normally rubbed could create a bit of excess gas, I'm sure every masseur in the Southern Hemisphere has witnessed that but an erection, a lob on, a stiffy (we used to play a game once, how many words you could think of for a stiff penis - try it, there really are tonnes - you can also try it with mammary glands etc) - now that would be a massive embarrassment, something you could imagine being played over in the masseurs staff room over a ginger tea and under the breath sniggers as you walk past for the rest of your stay.

For the males out there, you'll appreciate the predicament: men can get erections for reasons wholly non sexual, it can literally pop up when you don't expect it. Indeed, being completely honest with you, I've been caught out in several untoward places: dentist chairs, handing out papers in school as a pupil being probably the worse, when hormones were flying about everywhere and it seemed that your new little plaything was Erect more than often that it were Soft.

I'm eating curried prawns for breakfast with a delicious spicy bread filed with chilli and potato. On a nearby table an Indian man is eating Ricicles - those frosted rice crispies created as an alternative to Frosties for those who didn't like flakes, I kid you not. You always want what you haven't got.

One of the waiters, a man whose age it is difficult to guess, with a moustache that is surely stuck on from some joke shop

Please Don't Take Me Home - A Cat Called Robson-Kanu

in Trivandrum (the main town near here). He looks like Diego Costa and asks if my curry is spicy enough. I take this as a personal challenge, like he's daring me, questioning my masculinity - I'm eating prawn curry for breakfast for fucksake Diego is what I'm saying internally - smiling like a mad dog to his face. I could certainly do a bit more heat I suggest, snarling a little as I say it, signifying a toughness perhaps, that is really, if I care to admit, a load of old bollocks.

Diego smiles, it's one of those ominous grins he throws out before he's about to crack your Achilles with a rack of studs that makes contact stealth from the shadows behind Mike Deans back. He's a silent assassin and he's about to unleash chilli fury upon me and it's not even 8am. Bite it like this he suggests, cracking his massive gnashers expertly about the green stalk.

He eats it without any form of flinch. I flinch on his behalf. I haven't even eaten anything. He hands me the chilli. It's red, it's hot, it's going to give me the trots. I can almost hear the crowd singing the song.

I look at the thing. It's a fruit I'm sure. It's short, it's stubby - almost, like a fruity Sammy Lee.

I like to think of myself of being pretty metrosexual but there's an alpha male lurking in all of us, believe me, and at that moment it manifests itself in me grabbing a handful of these (5-7 is the best guess) of these, what I can best describe as tiny grenades of fruit destruction, and shamble them into my mouth, biting them and swallowing in one clumsy regrettable decision.

The pain was instant. It felt like I imagine it to feel if you were unlucky enough to be shot in the mouth from close range, and then survived, without any form of pain relief, watching your jaw hanging off with no opportunity of assistance as your tongue leaps out of your head like a rabid dog desperate for some of salvation.

I glimpse at faces around the room, drifting it feels in and out of consciousness, waiters, guests, the hotel fucking manager in pristine white cotton, probably harvested nearby, hovering over me like a young kestrel eager to understand what it is, this silly man in the Welsh grey 'away' kit has done to himself.

I seriously must pass out for when I wake, I'm in a room staring up at a fan, rotating clockwise I notice, some net curtain drifting in and out of this room on a breeze that must be rolling off the sea that I notice, even from where I lie, is gently washing over a beach I vaguely recognise.

To my left, a painting of a fishing scene, a port where tuna are dragged from a series of improbably beautiful boats, men pulling them to the shore where women take over and place them in crates. I have no idea where I am.

"How you feeling?"

A man comes into view from the door to my right wearing a pale blue uniform again probably from cotton; he takes my pulse whilst checking a wrist watch. I feel like I'm in a Bollywood version of Holby City – where's Connie Beachem (*1) when you need her?

Please Don't Take Me Home - A Cat Called Robson-Kanu

"How long have I been asleep for?" I ask.

He looks up at a clock on the wall, between two pictures predictably of Ganesh. There's also a print of the Taj Mahal and a line of elephants all dressed up, about, it seems to go into one jumbo sized battle.

"It's been a good 14 hours" he responds.

I've never slept 14 hours in my life. I've had some form of food poisoning he says and the chillies were what brought it out. He looks at me like I'm some form of problem – as if I have issues. Connie Beachem wouldn't look at me like that. She'd be sympathetic, I'm pretty sure.

"You ate seven of the birds eye hybrid chilli pepper; they're very potent" he says, concentrating on his vowels, completely not smiling. He actually looks angry – a bit like the doctor in A & E treating the man who's inadvertently sat (as you do) on a Henry the Hoover suction tube as he was cleaning the stairs, wasting valuable NHS resources – it's not something that should be joked about.

"You were and I hope you don't me saying this sir, but very silly" concentrating again on his vowels so the word 'silly' is drawn out and comes out like he has a major lisp. I nod and agree and apologise and feel a bit like I did in 1986 when I sliced Mark Williams' arm with a pencil sharpener blade who when he went to the nurse at the end of double history she stitched it up and when she asked how this was done, he said he caught it on a fence at lunchtime. She knew he was lying but respect for him covering for me - no surprise he became a marine. Tough character. Thank you Bungy, although you did get in some retaliation; the scar of my hand reminds me of that.

The man says I can go back to my room now and that I must drink lots of water and keep out of the sun, again, concentrating too much on the 's.'

"Go easy on the alcohol as well" he urges, headmaster like, again, not smiling.

I go back to my room, shower and we head to the restaurant where some passers by ask about how I'm feeling and I recognise them briefly from their stares as I lay in a chilli mess on the restaurant floor.

"I'm fine, really fine" I assure them all before embarking on a very bland dinner, involving perhaps not surprisingly no chilli whatsoever. Anyhow, a woman who yesterday briefly had introduced herself outside the place they do spa treatments, from Leicester but with North Indian descent, commented on how she had seen me doing Yoga in a Welsh kit and was keen to point out that one of Leicester's premier winning team had been part of the Wales team that made it to the semi finals.

She was very proud of Leicester as it goes; keen to remind me of their 5000-1 title success, against all the odds, she reassured together with Mark Selby winning the World Snooker Championship (yawn) and Leicester Tigers coming second in the Rugby. And that was without Richard the Fucking Third turning up in a Leicester car park. She really did love Leicester.

She said Wales had done great and obviously Andy King, their midfielder, was part of it she reminded me. I considered at one juncture that she might have a Jamie Vardy face tattooed on her lower torso and that this delicious breakfast I was trying to devour was somehow linked in some way to Leicester and Gary Lineker's market stall that she in all honesty, reminded me was in the centre of Leicester.

She said she supported Wales when England were knocked out and it's right that we all support each other right? I looked at her funny. I said it straight. No, that's not how I see it I said, totally smacking her, right between her eyes, like a bindi - look it up, it's a great metaphor considering.

No, you'll find most Welsh people and probably Scots for that matter and definitely the Irish, they really would support a rabid dog over England; in fact, if there were a team managed by Saddam Hussein, captained by Idi Amin and a squad consisting of players from Isis, ETA and the Provisional IRA, coached by Donald Trump and Nigel Farage and you were forced to support one team, let me tell you, it wouldn't, whilst I have a breath in my body, be England.

She said the thing with Iceland was a bit disrespectful though. I said I didn't think so and even that great English stalwart and pain in the arse Alan 'the record scoring goal scorer in the history of the universe' Shearer agreed that it was fine and again I surmised, there is, without going too deeply into it, quite a lot of history behind it.

Andrew Foley Jones

I tried to say this in a respectful tone and I'm not sure if I succeeded but she didn't mention Leicester again and said she hoped we did well in the World Cup Qualifiers and wished me well with my breakfast and disappeared towards her bungalow. I've been to Leicester I thought about saying, and it's really, quite nice I thought about adding, but didn't.

As I dipped the bread into the curried chillies I wondered whether this anti English thing went beyond decency - was I as bad as dare I say a Millwall supporting racist, a Russian Ultra from frozen Tbilisi, a right wing fascist from Dortmund with a swastika tattooed on his testicles. Like a good and bad cheese sandwich, there's a fine line between patriotism and nationalism.

The sky is filled with a flock of chattering crows and it's like they're searching out a rival gang of sea eagles or red falcons (*2) and I'd favour the birds of prey any time of the year if you asked me and the crows dive and bomb for a while, pick at some left over mango at a beach side sun lounger and then, still hungry for the fight, disappear into the crimson sunset.

I watch the waves crashing in, the artful power of the silver grey water creasing along the shoreline, boom, then over again and again, an eroding elegance and power; a beautiful destroyer - an oxymoron of nature viewed throughout the natural world. Identity is I gather, a good thing: a pride in what you are, where you have come from.

The next morning I go for my next Yoga session. The Yogi holding his hands in a prayer like way bids me good morning

and congratulates me on my victory against York. I couldn't believe it. He knows everything about everything.
"Good to see your full backs contributing."

I say, wearing my Welsh football kit (*3) "excuse me?" It was I suppose, a form of question. He eyes my Welsh crest, as so many passers by did indeed in France in the summer – it was probably a snapshot of what it must be like to be a woman with men drooling shamelessly over their breasts. He stretches his hands in an arch above his head. A coconut wobbles in the tree above; a chorus of cicadas chirrups to a crescendo and then, as quickly as it begins, it ends, leaving complete silence.

"Yes, I'm always of the view that whilst yes, of course, you definitely need a twenty goal a season striker, there's no doubt in my mind, that goals from across the side is what makes the difference at the end of the day, between play offs, or dare I say it, a championship winning side."

I am truly flabbergasted, a word that is by the way, way too underused. You could knock me down with a jack fruit or a coconut, which is statistically more likely you might be surprised to learn than winning the lottery, dying in a plane crash or as I alluded to earlier, being eaten alive by any form of shark.

"I mean, if you can have a few being fired in by full backs, midfielders, defenders as well as your strikers, then hell (yes a Yogi said the word hell), you're surely on a sure fire journey to promotion."

He has a point and something Wales perhaps need to work on. The over reliance on the goals of a certain Gareth Bale needs to be avoided if at all possible although saying that, there were some notable others who contributed in France.

"I agree, although don't let Phil Hardy hear you" I smile; he doesn't get that, but it is to be fair, pretty hard core – any Wrexham faithful of a certain age will recall the days of Phil Hardy which was the era before full backs dashed up and down the touch line – I don't think I ever saw him go beyond the half way line. I'm sure he scored one goal in a fairly meaningless penalty shoot out in the Welsh Cup or LDV Freight Cup or whatever it was called.

"How the fuck does you know all this" I actually say out loud, my English definitely poorer for speaking to Indian waiters all day and that by the way, is by no means meant to be racist. It is a factual statement; their English is patchy and yes, better than my Urdu.

"You'll know better than me" he continues "but you're clearly in need of a proven striker; or is that the chances just aren't being created?"

It's like reading Red Passion.

"Well I've been to all the home games, apart of course from the York game and obviously I watched the Dagenham and Redbridge debacle on television, at the airport in fact, when travelling out here but we seem to be solid enough at the back what with this Tilt who is nothing short of a Revelation and then there's Hamaz who whilst a little prone to the odd, do you know the expression 'brain fart' (he nods, half smiling) and whilst Riley looks a bit ring rusty I think he'll come good and then we've got solid enough full backs. But it's the midfield and the forward line where I think the problem lies."

He nods.

"You never appear to have found a replacement for Darren Ferguson" he suggests, almost whispering such could the truth of the statement affect me in a negative way.

"You're so spot on Yogi."

He closes his eyes and does that Indian thing again where they wiggle their heads from side to side (and before you say I'm racist, come to India, Indian people do it a lot by their own admission).

"You need a playmaker; someone who can control the rhythm of a game, someone who can play in a striker with a slide rule pass."

"Fuck Yogi. Can I fly to back to Wrexham and introduce you to Gary Mills."

I can't believe I'm swearing at a spiritual guru. He shrugs, reading perhaps my thoughts. What I and perhaps he are thinking, is, our manager doesn't possess the humility, the willingness to listen.

"Everybody needs a midfield general, a Scott Green, a Peter Ward, a Mike Lake (before he signed permanently of course)."

I nod wistfully, remembering the snowy day in Bury when Mike Lake had headed back to Sheffield I think it was and a sixty year old Jimmy Case of Liverpool Legend, took his place and shambled his way through ninety minutes of utter, unadulterated woe.

Mike Lake incidentally returned and signed permanently but rumour had it, he became somewhat pre occupied by spending his signing on fee rather than reproducing the form he has displayed whilst on loan.

"Often the case" agreed Yogi, nodding like one of those Chinese ornamental cats.

"I fear, and I caveat this as I don't know the man, but from what I see and hear and feel, I don't think it would do much good. I think Mr Mills knows his own mind which is often not a bad thing but only when decisions are in the main, correct ones. My concern is that perhaps he is from a different era and has not perhaps, you might say, encompassed the New World Of Modern Football."

He says it like it's a football manual that everybody needs to read with chapters on the offside rule, deliberate handball, 442 or 352 or heaven forbid The Christmas Tree Formation.

"I fear you might be right" I whisper back "I fear you might be right, although he has played a little more forward thinking in the last couple of games which is encouraging as setting out at home in particular with a solitary striker and a deep sitting

midfield is absolutely unacceptable in any league in any part of the world."
"Agreed" responds Yogi, high fiving me and then telling me to sit cross legged with my palms open to the heavens.
"Let's get that negative energy out of you" he urges.

Amen to that.

I suppose at this point of proceedings it would be apt for me to introduce a little about myself and the others who appear in this book.

I'm born in St Asaph and grew up in the North Wales coastal town of Prestatyn from where in the late 1970s a coach used to take people from the locality the thirty five miles or so to what would become my very own theatre of dreams, the Racecourse Ground, Wrexham.

I attended the local junior and comprehensive schools and dreamt of being a professional footballer (my dad was a semi pro, combining jobs like working for British Rail and Prudential Life Insurance with the relatively lucrative supplement of a local footballers wage) whilst mum worked in many jobs, such as on the General Post Office and in our local Sports Centre where I hanged out as a kid, playing five a side where somebody didn't turn up, or squash or table tennis or pool with the local reprobates who taught me all the swear words I could ever want to know. I also once stole a candy shrimp when she worked in the kiosk looking over the sports hall balcony: it was the only ever time I shoplifted – sorry mum.

My sister, five years my senior was hot property at our school and if I had a wayward moral compass, I could have sold photographs to those who seriously placed their orders with me. Scumbags – you know how you are. After leaving school and attending University she inadvertently met at local hot spot 'The Downtown' in Rhyl and soon after, married the lead singer of North Wales Rock Band The Alarm and from the age of 13 I grew up surrounded by the world of touring, concerts, recording studios, rock stars staying over with us. It was all I suppose pretty surreal.

I would hang out at gigs and as I got older sell t shirts, carry equipment, even tour manage during my university holidays which would often spill into term time. We would have visitors such as Billy Duffy, the archetypical lead guitarist from super group The Cult who would stay at our place whilst recording an album with Mike, during a collaboration called Colour Sound which should have gone onto really great things. If you get the chance, check out their only self titled album. It's a fantastic listen. It really is.

Billy was and still is, a massive Manchester City supporter. This you should remember was back in the day before the Emirati money had found its way to Moss Side and City still plied their distinctively average trade at the wonderfully atmospheric Main Road with its Kippax End where proper footballing characters shouted out banter that you rarely find in today's template shopping mall football grounds.

City were improbably, playing their football in League One, as incredibly were Wrexham. To think how both clubs have gone in separate directions since is truly amazing. Almost as amazing was Billy Duffy turning up at The Racecourse one Boxing Day and watching City unfairly beat us one nil, probably to a header to the beanpole that was Shaun Goater, opening up a Tupperware box crammed with turkey and cranberry sandwiches which we munched on as the game played on in the background. People in the main stand couldn't quite understand what would bring such a musical rock god to our humble ground. He incidentally enjoyed his day out and still follows our results. Remember that, when you hear those massive riffs off She Sells Sanctuary playing out.

Anyhow, I'm jumping ahead: the establishment where we would assemble on Sandy Lane, Prestatyn was called, you wouldn't believe it, The 69 Club. As a 6 year old I had absolutely no idea of the significance of that magical number. The adults obviously did.

My dad eventually took me and I would sit and watch the North Wales countryside pass by; the noise of men, a blur of things I didn't understand and didn't care about. I would look out for landmarks, roundabouts, the pub in Hope, Caergwrle and then the onwards stretch towards my new Mecca.

The first time I saw those lights was a real moment; it literally took my breath away and still ersatzly does. Remember in these days Wrexham were playing in what is now the equivalent of the Championship against sides such as Chelsea, Newcastle, West Ham, Swansea, Hull and even would you believe it, those giants of world football, Leicester City, Gary Walkers Match Of The Day Lineker, him of the famous Leicester Fruit and Vegetable Fame.

The noise was breathtaking, the smell of Bovril, hot dogs, Germolene from the players calves, the click of the turnstile, the sliding tackles of a certain Joseph Jones, the wing play of Steve Fox, the guile of Mel Sutton, the goals of that machine, Dixie McNeil.

It was a Right Of Passage and despite the barren years of disappointment, I really wouldn't swap it for the sterile world of the Premier League for whilst the product is lovely and pristine and the football a pleasure to sometimes indulge in, it isn't real, it's I suppose, to use a rather raw analogy, like a pair of Jordan's tits: quite nice to look at but soon it would just feel like grabbing a bowl of Rowntree's jelly.

Norwich City at home was my first game. We lost 3-1. Perhaps the writing was on the wall all the way back then.

But no, there are great memories, going ahead at Old Trafford, beating Arsenal obviously, the European adventures, Porto, Roma, Zaragoza, Anderlecht, Lyngby, watching Wales being England (oh the joy of joys), Mark Hughes' Scissor Kick in a 3-0 Demolition of the Spanish.

You wouldn't swop them for a single Premiership title.

So whilst there have been many times I've gone on record as saying for Fucksake dad, why the fuck did you not take me to say Old Trafford or Anfield on that fateful misty September night in 1979, overall, I must say thank you and thank you to The 69 Club for introducing me to the wonderful world of real, grass roots, unfranchised football.

Anyhow, back to the story - it's the day after Maidstone away. I'm finishing my Yoga with a particularly hamstring - cracking stretch that involves one leg pointing towards Australia, the other Albania. The one facing Albania is at crisis point; it's about to spring back like one of those slinky toys you used to throw down the stairs in the eighties.

I'm being told by Yogi to hold the pose for ten more seconds; you're going to have a broken hamstring on your conscious is all I can tell myself as I stare off into the HB2 leaden sky as I hear, I swear, a Slovakian woman who is also doing the session this morning, slips out a silent but deadly that is betrayed by an simply awful stench of chilli cabbage - fusion cooking - you wouldn't believe what experimentation can do with an Eastern Europeans insides.

I'm in too much discomfort, no discomfort is way too tame; I'm at fucking breaking point - I don't know if I've vicariously pissed off the Yogi by Mills refusing to revert to a simple 442 but he's seriously testing my tendons.

At last, he tells us to Ressssssssssstttttttt whilst shutting his eyes and pointing his palms towards the sky, a gesture that me and the Slovakian follow and as I concentrate on allowing junk to tumble from my mind and think of nothing but the energy of nature and the rock and the ocean and the trees and the sun and the wind that is thankfully percolating around us to extinguish the terrible aromas being produced by the anus of the Slovakian who, as I sneak a look over, is I swear pushing another one out as she mediates. Poor form.

We end the session and I resist the temptation to brag about our 2-1 victory in our opening group game, something I think the Yogi has given some thought to as he says without prompting as she walks, probably farting with every footstep, into the canopy of the forest:

"Respect In Victory is as important as Respect In Defeat" he declares as he folds up his exercise mat and hands me a glass filled with the juice of a watermelon, its seeds gently bobbing on the meniscus of this fine fluid.

"Did you see the result?" I ask.

"You really need to ask? is his repost.

He's clearly affronted by my suggestion, heaven forbid that he might not be aware of a result in The National League - he clearly watches a lot of football, I'll give him that.

"He just doesn't seem to be capable of adapting" is the first thing he says, gently, with an edge of regret and foreboding about his tone, not unlike the wind that is now growing heavier, picking up the fronds of palm trees; coconuts and jack fruits jangling uneasily in their pods.

The surf of the sea grows louder, higher, the swirls of grey and silver and white infiltrating the grey blue, swelling now, different torrents and channels colliding into each other producing huge up spouts of sea spray. Two women in colourful shawls sit on the headland: it would make a beautiful photograph.

"Adapting to what?" I say, understanding the answer,

perhaps, without needing to ask the question.

"You know deep down - a football club, a business, any organisation in fact, has to be the most important thing, more important than any player, any coach, any manager. If the ego of one individual is allowed to obstruct progress of that organisation, then you can have a major problem on your hands."

It's obvious what he's trying to say: Gary Mills needs to fuck right off.

"The sports science, the nitration, the statistics, the analysis, the scouting; these are the good things - the things that you simply cannot do without if you want to be successful."

"Exactly, the analogies are endless: a hospital not purchasing the latest radiology units, a factory refusing to use computers, a football club buying its players Dominos Pizza on the way back from an away game. I mean, Dominos, can you believe it?"

He laughs, sticking two imagery fingers down an imaginary throat indicating the international sign language for vomiting.

This Yogi is more westernised than I had given him credit for.

The metaphor this wise man is perhaps applying to the manager of my great and proud club is that he needs to look skywards and indulge in the positive changes that undoubtedly are taking place in the modern world to supplement those values that are perhaps better from a previous generation in an attempt of reaching a footballing position of Zen.

He says that Funny Old Game and Barton Bank and Atticus Finch are characters and that Sparky throws in the occasion gem and that Rob needs to keep an eye on Foxy (*4).

He also says, despite the good work the volunteers are putting in, it should, never be an excuse for not delivering excellence in every aspect of the business, from the fullness of the soap dispensers in the Mold Road Stand to the temperature of the pies in the Tech End to the way the stewards interact with the away supporters, meagre as it typically is.

"To be successful, you have to be forever professional" he sermons.

"I swear you get these from calendars or Christmas crackers" I suggest.

"I don't do calendars or Christmas" is his response.

The next thing that happens is as unbelievable as it is bizarre. On the beach besides the Yoga stage, a number of jackfruits have fallen from the forest. Eleven in fact; and the crazy thing is, the jackfruit, big bloated orange fruits that you will know or guess, grow high up in the trees.

Well, before this gets too Richard Attenborough, the whole point of this part of the story is that the jackfruit have assembled, in the yellow sand in a perfect four by four formation with a goalkeeper sitting behind it, twigs from a palm tree, marking out a football pitch with goals either end, two penalty boxes compete with the little box players have to queue around when there's a penalty, centre circle, penalty spots created by two quartz threaded pebbles. We didn't need to say it but we did anyway, in compete unison:

"It's surely a sign: Gary, please please play it easy - 442 is the way forward."

A sea eagle swoops down, the sea relents, waves gently abating, the grey storm clouds that had gathered above the horizon disappeared into a milky blue marble sky, a yellow frisbee of a sun appearing throwing heat and hope across the forest, across the beach, across the land.

"It's I suppose difficult to reconcile being happy with a drawn game away, at, and, no disrespect, Maidstone United."

He rests his palm against my shoulder. He feels my pain, I can feel the empathy passing through my body.

"I know, I know - I mean, it must be so difficult with what having such a decent history and what, only twenty years ago, your fans could accurately sing 'One Team In Wales' and genuinely mean it. Christ, when you see what Cardiff and I mean, obviously particularly Swansea have achieved over the last decade and it must really, well, rankle with you all."

It's amazing how perceptive this man of elastic actually is:

could he be a contender for the manager's job once we oust this fraud Gary Mills.

"Small twists of fate, lightning moments and things can go this way and that" before adding, "and your bad luck was those (name removed for legal reasons) characters getting involved with the club and seriously stripping away the very bones of the club."

I nod, I may even allow a tear to pass along my cheek.

"Football has become the plaything of the rich and famous; it's a shame how it has forgotten itself. I mean, I can't bring myself to watch a premier league match any more. It's just full of how do you say, cow shit?"

"You're close enough" I smile.

"And that percolates through the divisions, I mean what about the 98 point season, you should be winning any league with 98 points but hey, Fleetwood come along with their wealthy owner, and buy your best players and hey, effectively win the league. And you can't really blame Mangan and of course that wasted talent Lee Fowler: money talks when you've got a mortgage and a family – of course it does but deep down, I think we all know it - it's just not what sport is all about."

You're so right. You're so right. I am crying now. All this fresh air and the head massages and the chilli and these words of such wisdom– it's bringing out years of footballing despair.

"But it's how it is now and until some sense prevails and some rules are changed, it's what we're stuck with. It's perverse in my view. It hits right in the very face of the ideals of sport."

I wonder how I would feel if a sugar daddy, a benefactor, an investor, call it what you want, came along and ploughed his hard earned gains in the football club. Would I complain as we smashed the economic equilibrium and bought in the best players on the best contact packages? Would I complain as we climbed the leagues?

I'd like to think I would appreciate it was not what sport is about; I'd like to think I would be gracious enough to realise that such victories would effectively be hollow and empty and as I passed the trophy cabinet and the photographs depicting our new found glory on the concourse walls, I genuinely feel it wouldn't satisfy me.

I think about my friend Davy Boy, a nicer man you could not meet. He supports Chelsea and has done for years, even when they were shit. I ask him how he felt when Roman Abramovich came along and sunk his new capitalist billions into the, club, bringing almost instant success. He says he liked it at first but now it just feels somewhat wrong.

The same applies no doubt to Man City moving from the shadows of Moss Side, to an empty part of, town in their new complex, everything feels a bit like it's in a huge shopping mall in Dubai or Qatar. It feels lacking in substance. Empty. Soulless.

At our level it's becoming more common: look at Forest

Green Rover, Eastleigh, Dover and even in the leagues below – FC Fylde for Fucksake, throwing money around like it's confetti at a wedding.

"Good luck for promotion: you deserve to be back in the league" he said, smiling as warmly as my scolded feet.
He walks away and I look back at the beach and the sea and a thousand colourful fishing boats, drifting along the ocean towards the nearby harbour and fishing market where women with baskets await the return of their men and the nets; such a noble trade.

I close my eyes, listening to the sound of the surf crashing over the beach. I think back to June and as I said at the beginning, recall the story of that glorious month.

This is the simple story of two friends who journeyed to watch their team, simply expecting some fun, the once in a generation opportunity to watch their nation at a sporting event but who incredibly ended up against all odds, watching their team reach the semi finals.

Please Don't Take Me Home - A Cat Called Robson-Kanu

THE BEGINNING: OCTOBER 2015

I've woken up with a xylophone in my bed, a pig head in my refrigerator with cherries on sticks where the eyes should be and a man in his underpants eating Golden Graham's straight from the packet.

I ask him to leave and as he does, a woman appears from the hallway cloakroom and she's wearing my Wrexham away kit worn by the Maverick playmaker Glen Little no less which I ask her to take off, averting my eyes as she does this putting on a top that the man with the cereal box gives her. I must admit to an inadvertent glance of part of her left breast; I'm only human after all.

I notice on my painting of my JJ Adams 'The Queen' (an ironic dig at the monarchy), someone has added a fake moustache and I picture this and tweet it, immediately gaining 14 favourites, 8 retweets. I check my Facebook post from last night which simply said 'Nos Da Pawb' and this generated 78 likes - not bad.

On E Bay, I glance at the watched item of a Wrexham programme in 1979, my first game, a 3-1 loss to Norwich City. Still £2.50. Then an All Saints man bag, some Diesel jeans, a pair of shoes by Russell and Bromley.

Once I've checked my e mail, Face book, Twitter, What's App, I shower and dress: jeans, a t shirt, my lucky football leather jacket - the usual kit.

I check on Red Passion and read Funny Old Game winding

up some characters and there's Foxy questioning ambition and Sparky punning like a pun King. I've not posted on there for some time; I used to be fairly prolific. I even used to start some threads of my own: Neil Salathiel is a Salamander, the Enigma that is Patrick Suffo, Henry The Hoover Is A Wrexham Fan.

Mark Beck, our new striker is getting lambasted, Gary Mills the Wrexham manager getting criticised for playing players out of position; reports of Grey, Hudson and York being on the piss again in Chester and true enough, I did spy them in the Commonhall Social the other night having a few on a school night. Wasted talent is a silly thing. You know, if you play football yourself, can you imagine how much you'd give if you were a professional. I'm not saying any of these would have made it at a higher level but give yourself a chance. Drinking a couple of nights before a game is simply unacceptable: disrespectful, foolish, wasteful.

I walk down to the car where Andrew Kinsella is waiting to take me to the football, noticing the couple from the fifth floor penthouse are looking at me with something of an odd look. We're playing Woking or Dover or maybe Grimsby, I've lost track. They're walking a tiny dog that could actually be a cat; really don't see the point of tiny dogs but each to their own. And no, I won't be attending the Residents Association Meeting; I'm washing my hair or something.

I open the door and as ever he's on the phone. He eventually kills the call, looks across at me and laughs as I pull across my seat belt in his sleek yet functional Audi. There a half eaten Double Decker in the footwell, the latest edition of Haulage

Monthly and an invite to some christening.

Who we playing today?

No idea?

What kind of fan are you?

Maybe Grimsby.

Big fish.

Or Woking or Dover.

Not so big.

He asks me if I'm excited about France.

Of course.

You'll get knocked out in the group though; you get that right?

Go fuck yourself.

He laughs again.

What you laughing at?

Rough night?

Pretty much.

Andrew Foley Jones

You might want to check out your boat race.

He's recently moved to London; I've bought him a book on rhyming slang. He's coming out with stuff like frog and bone, Tiddly Winks, and other stuff I think people are making up, mocking him.

I pull down the cosmetic mirror and glance up at my face; on my forehead it says, in plum lipstick, possibly by Chanel or Max Factor a word that shouldn't ever be written across someone's face.

Cheeky bastards. What a violation. Surely there must be something in the UN Convention about writing on the face of a fellow human being. The fact that I was in such a state to allow someone to do this is nether here nor there.

Do you have any of those wipes woman take make off with?

You mean make up wipes.

That's it.

The thing girls use to wipe off their make up?

Or Eddie Izzard?

Yeah, or Eddie Izzard.

Have a look in the glove compartment.

Fair play, amongst the half eaten bag of Revels (does

Please Don't Take Me Home - A Cat Called Robson-Kanu

anyone like the coffee ones), a tape measure, a box of Tampax, a yo yo and a pen that has Baltimore written down its side with a woman who's bikini falls away as you tilt the pen downwards; and sure enough there's some make up removal wipes by Boots.

I flip open the cosmetic mirror on the back of his sun flap and wipe off the graffiti from my face. The defamation has been removed.

We cross the border and pass a Gwynedd Shipping truck and he tells me to take a picture and tweet it: he's the Managing Director and still loves the thrill of seeing one of his trucks on the UK's motorway system.

We pass south along the A483 and I feel the instant buzz of pride and anticipation as we take the Wrexham turnoff and at the Sainsburys roundabout, the lights loom large, metallic silver against the marble blue sky. We park up at the Maesgwyn Hall and pay our £3

We meet in The Turf, a pub that if you're not a Wrexham fan is magically lodged within the actual curtilage of the actual stadium itself. It used to be that the chosen few could watch a game from the balcony that used to overlook the pitch before the new stand was built. The Turf is a great pub; adorned with paraphernalia from Wrexham's glorious past with an incredible match day atmosphere, even here, in the darkest days of our footballing history.

We meet the usual crew, Glyn, Mark, Steve, Paul, Frank - people I have literally met by attending games - friendships formed through going to the match. Ninety minutes every other week, relationships built over the seasons: small talk evolving to deeper conversations about all aspects of daily life.

We've now clubbed together and hired a box for the season: it's a great place to watch, right on the half way line and it helps support the club. And before anyone says it, it's not a contradiction to what I've been critiquing earlier about how football has become so corporate: this really isn't the prawn sandwich type of place to watch football that Roy Keane so wonderfully parodied in his fantastic autobiography. We're just a group of mates who decided it would be fun to club together and watch the game together with a nice view over the half way line with a little place to have a cup of tea at half time (don't I repeat ever go for a coffee, if there's one thing I can't do is drink shit coffee and the coffee at Wrexham is unbelievably shit).

We head off to the game; I won't bore you with the minutiae but Wrexham played Grimsby and there were no goals; and I guess if they were still playing today, there's still be no goals.

Grimsby have since been promoted and we've well, you've guessed it, languished in a state of near suspended terminal decline. I have the job of writing about it in the Daily Post, a publication that you from the north and mid Wales will be familiar with. It's a decent newspaper although some question whether they get into the real dirty nooks and cracks of the football club when the need really arises.

Anyhow, that's another story; the point to note, and to be

fair, this could have related to many games at the time and certainly over this season. The inertia during that game was palpable; and perhaps a metaphor for the wider demise - the whole place stinks of rotting, decaying tedious inertia and all I could do was pan around the crumbling Kop, the faded seats in the stands opposite and weep for how far we've fallen.

Football fans are the only people who come back to view a form of entertainment regardless of the fact, it is highly likely to be really shite. I love my club and I crave so much to be climbing up the leagues and when I look at people like Bournemouth and Swansea, it fills me with some hope but today, I return home feeling a deep despair: watching fifth tier football is pretty dire but when it's in your blood, you can't turn your back.

This is a bit of scene setting, the people who teach creative writing call it: the above sets out that I like drinking, watching football and that I've been both cursed and blessed with supporting Wrexham FC and being Welsh. I'm unashamedly proud of both. I say cursed in the sense that success has been fairly limited.

There's a couple of stand out moments: beating Arsenal of course, winning a couple of promotions, going ahead at Old Trafford, beating Porto, nearly beating Zaragoza, Wales being on the edge of qualification on so many heartbreaking occasions.

I've always been hugely proud of my nationality but in sporting terms, I've not been blessed with success. Wales qualifying for a major tournament is something I've been craving of for a long time and I feared it would be something that would evade me. The only thing that could ride it close would be Wrexham in the Premiership. You might think it's the dream of a mad man but who knows?

The season ends limply, Wrexham don't make the play offs but there's talk about a new lease on the Racecourse Ground so we'll start again next season awash with optimism and dreams.

I turn my attention to the summer in France. This is a story of our journey. Most of the below did actually happen. The identities of some have been changed; you know who you are.

This is ultimately the story of an underdog, a group of players and its supporters who dared to dream, stuck together and ended up having the time of their lives.

THE WELSH NATIONAL ANTHEM

(First stanza)
Mae hen wlad fy nhadau yn annwyl i mi,
Gwlad beirdd a chantorion, enwogion o fri;
Ei gwrol ryfelwyr, gwladgarwyr tra mad,
Dros ryddid collasant eu gwaed.

(Chorus)
Gwlad, gwlad, pleidiol wyf i'm gwlad.
Tra môr yn fur i'r bur hoff bau,
O bydded i'r hen iaith barhau.

(Second stanza)
Hen Gymru fynyddig, paradwys y bardd,
Pob dyffryn, pob clogwyn, i'm golwg sydd hardd;
Trwy deimlad gwladgarol, mor swynol yw si
Ei nentydd, afonydd, i mi.

(Chorus)

(Third stanza)
Os treisiodd y gelyn fy ngwlad tan ei droed,
Mae hen iaith y Cymry mor fyw ag erioed,
Ni luddiwyd yr awen gan erchyll law brad,
Na thelyn berseiniol fy ngwlad.

Andrew Foley Jones

JUNE 2016: LEG 1 – TRAVELLING TO BORDEAUX

Travelling around France in June of 2016 was a bit like that cartoon 'The Wacky Races.' I've travelled around in all forms of transport. I know the transport links of France like the back of my proverbial hand. It started with an early bird taxi from Chester: we were then supposed to get to France like this:

5:10am flight from Manchester to Paris.

9:35am train from Charles de Gaulle airport, Paris to Orly airport to the south of Paris.

12:35 flight from Orly airport to Bordeaux.

At the airport there's the obligatory groups of stag dos, hen dos, people necking shots in the airport bar, a groom to be with a t shirt that says in blood red lettering LIFE TO SOON BE OVER, vomiting into a flower arrangement outside Pret A Manger and we decide to go for the civilised option and go for a coffee and a smoothie chaser is as risky as it gets (super fruit berry boost no less) with a side order of cranberry muffin.

There's a splattering of northern based Welsh supporters and instantly you feel a kinship with these strangers, just through the colours of their shirts, their Spirit of '58 memorabilia – the great retro replica kits and hats. We exchange nods and a quiet mutual respect born out of our great principality.

On the flight we catch up on the team news, read up on the violence that has already beset the tournament with England's notable fringe element causing mayhem in the south of France.

On the team news front everything seems in order and we attempt unsuccessfully a crossword, eight down leading to catastrophic failure and instead I search out Welsh related items on E Bay, a George Berry replica shirt being the most exciting of the items on display.

As we arrive in Charles De Gaulle, having only got hand luggage, we whizz through, only to be hit by a vast queue at passport control. At this point, I recall with some horror, Richard's irrational aversion to queues of any description: he won't mind me sharing this with you but he has an almost pathological issue with standing in any form of queue.

So to deal with this social disorder, he simply pretends the queue isn't there and walks, parallel to it with a confident stride and a clear purpose as to reach the man in the passport box before those patiently awaiting their turn.

I mention something about 'if everyone did this, anarchy would prevail' but his disorder eclipses any attempt at sense and as we soon hit our first hurdle on this obstacle course of social awkwardness – the obstacle is a man apparently from Germany who looks like he's attending a Sales Conference on Vacuum Cleaners or some form of Widget Convention and he's clearly so unimpressed at this blatant violation of Lining Up Etiquette that he's developed a terribly flushed complexion and I'm half expecting him to grab his right arm and collapse to the concrete floor, such is his rage.

I begin to placate him as he develops an almost purple tinge but Richard is not for stopping, as he bulldozers forward and says very forcefully: "please move aside - we're going to miss our connecting flight – we must go through."

I wonder if the maroon coloured Hoover sales man understands that we wouldn't need to go through Passport Control for a connecting flight but it seems to work and he stands to one side and the man's face restores a more ordinary tone and we head forward and reach our quarry - the man at Passport Control with no expression who greets us from his tiny box – a very claustrophobic place to spend your working day.

I wonder if it's a prerequisite for the job that you have to be a rude and miserable bastard or is it something you train up for. I mean, it's usually your first impression of the country you're visiting. You'd think they'd try and create a slightly more welcoming atmosphere.

We both ask The Miserable Bastard for a stamp in our passports, something that has become a bit of a competition over the years (sad I know) but we are forcibly denied our souvenir and Henri is not for messing with, his onward movement with his arm and his head tells us to keep going and we move forwards, looking back as we go at the incredibly long queue that snakes behind us.

Through the airport towards the train station and we find our platform and then note our train is already here and we're fannying around on the train, causing a decent amount of chaos, getting on the wrong carriage, sitting in someone's else's seats, the daft tourist routine getting us nowhere. It's like the Pulp lyric "everybody hates a tourist:" we're truly idiotic. If I were a local, I'd be calling us all sorts.

We scramble around and get off and just about make it onto the correct carriage and shambolically find where we should be. We settle into our seats which are gloriously first class and better than anything you would get in the UK. After all the fuss, we're only on it for about one hour and fifteen minutes; it seems a shame to get off it and then have a change of train and then get a bus to Orly airport.

Richard is in charge of transportation and me accommodation. His charge involves scouring the Internet for various forms of transport and linking them together. It's a high level of logistic task and I'm pleased he's taken it on.

My job is going on the Airbnb web site and taking a pop shot at a two bed apartment in the centre of the city we are staying in (Jonny Rogers will tell you I sometimes don't quite get it right but if a lady in Lithuania thinks 25 miles in soviet suburbia is city centre then I'm always going to be on to a loser).

I think he's got the sticky end of the stick but then, each to his own skill set. And to be fair, he is very good at organising trips: they don't call him Compass Head for nothing.

I look at the neon strip of destinations whizzing across a screen at the top of the carriage. The train to the airport goes directly to Bordeaux. It arrives ten minutes earlier than if we continued on our designated route via Orly.

"We might as well stay on the train" I suggest, trying not to hurt his feelings as despite the journey planning being a little shit, you can't criticise, especially on our inaugural trip.

It's been a long morning, having been collected at 4am from Chester by our soon to be chauffeur in waiting on several journeys to Manchester airport throughout the glorious month of June. Tony is a taxi driver who has learnt the knack to know when you want to converse and when you don't. I am so excited for any form of trip that I love to babble on to anyone who will listen. He's also an Englishman who isn't a complete prick. That's normally an oxymoron, a paradox, a dichotomy – you get the message.

I've hardly slept: last night I tried to get some action as it traditionally sends me off quite nicely but she was having none of it and eventually I dropped off, dreaming oddly of Margaret Thatcher mud wresting with the leader of North Korea. I'm not sure who won and what my therapist would say about it. I once went to North Korea with Darren Mercer but that's an altogether different story.

At the buffet cart I order a latté and a sandwich in broken French and the server tries to correct me and I smile and say 'oui' over and over, louder each time before finally holding out my hands and saying 'merci' in a gravelly voice.

As I sip on my cafe au lait I stare out of the window; a scarecrow in a field, some low industrial buildings, a stench of inertia, some schoolchildren idling around a set of red metal swings in a playground, graffiti along low oblong walls, a yellow balloon drifting through the pavement slab of a sky. I love watching landscapes unfold through a train window. A man on our carriage, reading some form of academic publication, starts talking broken English to us. He's far from friendly and points to the headline in his newspaper, sitting front page down on the Formica table, before him.

"England Bad" he says, directing us to a headline and photographs of general social disorder: Heineken bottles hurtling through the air, fat tattooed men kicking other slimmer men in the head. It really is quite sickening but we've seen it all before. He shakes his head and goes back to his book. Others on the train look at us in disdain. We're as popular as Donald Trump at a Hilary Clinton Thanksgiving Dinner.

I don't like people thinking I'm a wanker. I don't think that generally I am, but they are all labelling me and Richard as such and it doesn't feel good. It feels like we're being lambasted for something completely not of our making. It's a terrible miscarriage of social justice.

So to address the injustice, I stand and grab my bag from the overhead compartment and pull out a Welsh flag. I flutter it in front of us. I begin to hum the National Anthem. Ok, it's probably all a bit weird and these people are probably beginning to fear they're stuck with an odd one until the next station but the point I am trying to make and beyond turning into Tom Jones wearing a daffodil head, I couldn't do any more to say - hey people: look - we're not fucking English: we're fucking Welsh.

I hold up the flag again me and it dances theatrically in the afternoon breeze. There's an awkward pause, a bit like just before Donald Trump is about to speak or tweet or generally breathe. You just know something odd is going to happen. However, it does not – what happens is the people on the carriage, the man, the conductor all look slightly perplexed and then collectively break into a huge smile and then together, begin to clap, slow at first but then full blown, enthusiastic applause you might get at a children's nativity play or a Nigel Farage speech – warm and sincere enough:

"Ah, Pay De Galles" he says reaching out to shake our hand; the others on the carriage smiling too. It appears, the roast beef as the English are referred to, are due to their exploits in Marseilles, even less popular than ever and the analogies are as obvious as they are plentiful: Boris Johnson in an EU Summit, Mickey Thomas in a Countering Counterfeit Currency Conference etc.

"Oui" I say, "Pay De fucking Galles; not English."

"Roast Beef" shouts the man, holding his nose in the international renowned sign language for "this stinks."

Together, we all shout: "stinky roast beef."

We all laugh and through the window, a shaft of sunlight, a sign of things, perhaps, to come.

It's moments like these that being Welsh and not English is even sweeter than normal and I don't wish to appear small minded, parochial, dare I say racist, when I say that. I have a lot of English friends, I live in England for gods sake, there's a lot of good in England but unfortunately, I think it's fair to say, in their hoards of football supporters, they have a higher than average ratio of real knob heads.

We exchange small talk for the rest of the journey. He tells us he's doing an engineering course. He wants to work on a large dam project in Dubai. I say I would be a rubbish engineer. I couldn't even open my Meccano box when I was a kid; all I wanted to do was play football for Wrexham and Wales. I wrote a story about it when I was 9. I was obsessed with it.

The man lists everything he knows about Wales:

Prince Charles

Princess Diana

Coal Mines

Gareth Bale

Thistles

Rugby

Haggis

Tailless cats

Stonehenge

Stereophonics

Please Don't Take Me Home - A Cat Called Robson-Kanu

Catherine Zeta Jones

Ryan Giggs

I smile encouragingly and say 5 out of 12 isn't bad and I chink my glass of beer against his polystyrene coffee cup. I think about humming the French national Anthem but to be honest, I can't remember it - so instead I shout "Zinedine Zidane" and mime an imaginary head butt to his chest. He laughs and head butts me back. It turns out, not many people know much about our beautiful principality.

Outside, the beautiful French countryside passes by, fields in different shades of green and yellow and brown, lots more scarecrows, farmhouses, windmills, rolling hills, a town, an industrial estate, a slogan on a wall, people standing on a bridge looking down as we whizz on by, beneath them.

We approach Bordeaux and I feel like a small child, momentarily picturing myself back in the late 1970s/early 1980s in a snapshot in my Wales kit, the one Terry Yorath epitomised made by Admiral with the iconic yellow and green stripes.

I log into Red Passion: there's about as much transfer activity as a plate of samosas at a Donald Trump Campaign Buffet. We've pretty much got enough players to play a five a side match and I'd still fancy our chances. The way it's going this could be another really shit season.

I flick about Facebook, Twitter, read my e mails, check on the football programme on e bay, a pair of all saints shorts, the

Andrew Foley Jones

Welsh replica strip apparently worn by George Berry. God, there's some shit on here; you can genuinely buy anything (not that I am suggesting in any way, shape or form that anything relating to the wonderful George Berry is shit – he was a true stalwart – playing the game in an era where racism was rife and shameful).

I look along the carriage and everyone is on their devises and I ponder, what did we do before this. I can remember life before this and I suppose it's the same with every generation or even half generation but it really is a huge shift socially – think about it.

Don't get me wrong, the majority of what technology brings is wonderful but I can't help but think that it does make us a much more insular society. The interaction on the carriage was an enjoyable social moment. Sometimes we all need to make more of an effort.

As we pull into Bordeaux, we collect our cases from the compartment between the toilet and the door. I hear the noise of what I initially think is a small baby and then notice on the floor of the corridor, a little cage with a cat's ginger face appearing through the metal railings.

A woman appears, muttering something in French, struggling to carry some 1930s style luggage, a small boy by her side, wearing a t shirt with He Man And The Masters Of The Universe written on it.

I offer to carry one of her cases but she dismisses me with a pig like grunt and pulls her two pieces of luggage and the boy from the carriage, stumbling down the steps onto the platform.

I remain on the train, next to the cage with the cat, and shout to her whether she would like me to carry the cat off the train. She lingers in the door way, half shouting to the boy and then says something that sounds like "keep the cat, he likes you" before disappearing along the platform, the little boy turning back to me, waving, perhaps to the cat, rather than to me.

Some other passengers look into the cage and they alight and then a guard, says to me heavily accented, "if this is your stop, you must now leave the train; we must leave - you must take all your things" pointing to my bag and to the cat in the cage.

I sling my bag over my shoulder and grab the cage by the plastic handle on its top and awkwardly alight the train, nodding a hi to a couple in their glorious Welsh kits, the red somehow an indescribable colour, it's vibrancy and beauty, difficult to put into words.

The cat meows as we walk along the platform: his cry sounds somehow like a human voice: a line of graffiti right along a heavy wall, separating the station from a highway running on a bridge above; faces of cartoon superheroes, tags by local characters I picture wearing hoodies and caps; an urban sprawl that somehow fits in with its surroundings. I think briefly about discussions about whether graffiti is art or vandalism – I actually like it but I can see why some don't – another generational difference perhaps.

The cat says something, I swear. It sounds like "you're just a peninsula on the edge of England." I gesture to Richard, a gesture that perhaps says, what the fuck am I to do with this cat. He gestures back; a Gallic shrug that wouldn't look out of place in a Gerald Depardieu movie. Did you hear that I say to Richard who doesn't appear to have heard either me or the cat. I'm carrying a xenophobic French cat though Bordeaux station.

After another hundred metres of platform and accompanying graffiti covered walls and the cat repeating on a loop "you're just a peninsula on the edge of England" and I reach the ticket barrier and hand in my printed off sheet, that nowadays counts as a ticket and the conductor, a man called Thierry, ushers me through.

"This can is saying bad things to me" I say to Thierry. "He keeps saying stuff."

He Gallic shrugs back, telling me with a forward nod, to keep moving, to stop blocking the queue that I note is starting to develop, despite us being what I thought were one of the last off our carriage; I hadn't taken into account the double deck SNCF train with its chrome panels and overall much sexier appearance than our British Rail counterparts.

I head up some steps and past some vending machines, noticing a retro Pepsi cola billboard, spinning over now to Fanta Limon, then Camel cigarettes, a patch of blue sky, a jet idling overhead, a blast of horn from the highways, hanging above us.

Please Don't Take Me Home - A Cat Called Robson-Kanu

A woman in the mouth of the customer services section of the station looks down at the cat and smiles, a lovely sincere welcoming smile which is probably why she got the job. The cat purrs and says nothing.

I approach her and point to the cat. He looks up to me (I'm assuming it's a 'he') and I hear I swear him say something that sounds like "go fuck yourself." I look down and he looks like he's grinning at me.

She says in perfect English "pretty cat, what's its name?"

I shake my head.

"I don't know, I mean, it's not even my cat."

"What do you mean, it's not your cat?" she replies.

I shrug, not as Gallicly, I imagine as Depardieu, Richard or Thierry, but it's a genuine shrug nonetheless.

"I mean, it's not my cat" I respond.

"I don't understand" she says, a birthmark I notice, on the edge of her right ear.

"I mean" I shrug, "I found the cat on the train from Paris."

She frowns, and says: "ah I see."

"I'm here to watch the football" I say; "it's really not my cat. I don't even own a cat. There was Frisky One and Frisky Two but that's an altogether different story. I mean I just found the cat. There was a woman, a woman on the train, I think she owns the cat. She had a child and loads of vintage cases. She appeared to just leave the cat and I gestured her towards it but she just kind of half frowned, half smiled and walked away. It was like she was saying, I just don't want the cat."

The woman perhaps understands my manic monologue just a little and I smile and point towards the ginger kitten, its nose protruding through the barriers in the tiny cage.

"And it sounds mad, but the cat is saying stuff to me – bad stuff. He's actually quite racist."

She appears to ignore this, what I would deem to be pretty big relevant stuff and instead, as if coming across a talking racist cat is an every day occurrence in Bordeaux points to the crest on my Wales away kit:

"Where are you from?"

"Wales" I say.

"Is that part of England?" she asks.

We laugh and shake our heads.

We show her a map of the U.K. on my phone.

"Ah" she smiles.

Please Don't Take Me Home - A Cat Called Robson-Kanu

"Shirley Bassey?"

"Yes that's right."

"Hey big spender" she sings, grabbing Richard by the arm, dancing him around the platform.

"More Shakin' Stevens" I laugh, pointing at Richard's awkward movements, his messed up knees.

She takes my number and tells me she will find a home for the cat. She will let me know if she finds the owner she says.

I stroke the cat through the bars of the cage and it purrs sarcastically and I smile at the lady who picks up the case and a news notification on my phone of some shooting in America, a text message from Stephen Halpin wishing me luck, a reminder from e bay that the bidding on the George Berry shirt ends at 19:45.

I look down at the cat and he says: "Enjoy yourself – you know you won't make it past the group stages" before turning away and licking what might be his own testicles.

I look back and try and put this to the back of my mind: maybe it's the early start, maybe someone's dropped some acid in my coffee. The cat appears to be giving me the finger as we leave the station and I notice the first splattering of Welsh supporters dotted around a couple of bars outside the train station, others in a taxi queue which we join, soon finding a taxi. We ask him to take us to a destination that I show from a map on my phone. He holds it out and nods his head.

We've booked an Airbnb which says it has two bedrooms and is in the city centre. There's always an element of uncertainty when booking with Airbnb so we approach the apartment with a certain element of trepidation.

I call the owner and he soon appears, opening a heavy metal door, directing us into a beautiful industrial building and in broken English ushers us to follow him. We get to the first bend in the stairwell, up concrete steps and wait for him to open a nearby door. He however points upwards and we head up upwards, up to another turn and upwards again; after 78 steps we reach the apartment, hopelessly out of breath. It's been like the final ascent of Snowdon; unforgiving. I just hope the reward at the summit is worth it.

He opens the door and shows us around. It has a Juliette balcony looking over a street and a tram line, which as it says on the web site, runs right in front of the apartment block.

It's clean and there's a lounge with a shower but there's definitely only one bedroom. With Richard's legendary snoring problem, there's no way I'll be sharing a bed with him. I explain this to the owner. He pulls out a mattress and a pretty unimpressive duvet and pillow combination by way of a solution. It's covered in images from the French equivalent to my Little Pony which is a bit weird - it's not ideal but it's fine for what we need although I would have much preferred something like Garfield and Friends.

As he leaves, we open the wardrobes and cupboards and

they're full of every day stuff. It's clear that he ordinarily lives here and as he leaves, he explains he heads off to stay with his girlfriend whenever he gets a booking.

By all accounts this is a common theme in France where there are in fact more Airbnb lets than hotel rooms. House owners see it as a way of earning extra cash and it does feel pretty weird, a little like you're kicking them out of their house. His choice I suppose; no one made him do it.

As he leaves, he points to my crest and says "Angleterre."

"No, Wales," I shout.

"Ah, part of England" he says as he waves au revoir.

"No, definitely not part of England" I shout after him.

He turns back and winks, wiggles his hips and sings the introduction to The Green Green Grass Of Home, shouting "I love Tom Jones - I know that Wales is not in England - dumb ass" as he closes the door and heads off down the stairwell.

I think about opening one of his bottles of Kronenbourg but resist and instead, we have a quick wash and head off down the 78 steps into Bordeaux.

We follow the sound of singing and spot a group of Welsh supporters outside a pub called Sweeney Todd's. Inside we order some drinks and suddenly the pub is crammed with men and women in Wales replica kits, some draped in the Welsh flag. Soon, the first chorus of "don't take me home" blasts through the airwaves, each verse becoming louder and louder.

We learn the words (not a hugely tricky task) and join in, jostling with our fellow country men, exchanging greetings, tales of our individual journeys from the Principality. It's funny, but if you saw these people on a high street in Prestatyn, Pontypridd or Pwhelli, you probably wouldn't even look at them, but here, as a group, a minority, on a foreign soil, we have a collective commonality, a collective belief, something which binds us together, makes us want to communicate with each other, look out for each other. It's ultimately a good feeling, something that we should somehow carry through in our day to day lives, long after this tournament is over.

We occupy a table in the corner underneath a French flag and a picture of the Guinness Toucan with a speech bubble coming from its beaky mouth saying "A Guinness A Day Helps You Work Rest And Play."

The pub is rammed and we feel lucky to find a seat after our long day of travel. It soon becomes clear however why this area is clear; it's right next to the rest room where a line of Welshmen queue, singing as they wait patiently in line. After a couple of pints, the developing stench determines that we leave the Sweeney Todds and venture elsewhere into the heartland of Bordeaux.

Along the promenade we move from bar to bar, chatting to different people from all over Wales and Europe; it feels like a million Christmas Eves, it's the best night out ever.

After we take in a number of establishments, including a drunken selfie with Craig Bellamy, we venture home, up our 78 steps and into our respective places of sleep, he in his luxurious king sized bed, me on my mattress on the kitchen floor.

As he drifts into a sleep I lie awake, considering the half eaten Pringle parallel to my head beneath the refrigerator, it's steady hum creating a night time industrial soundtrack that soon, intermingles with the passing of a tram and then the wonderful overtones of the Welsh National Anthem drifting through the street. There's something beautifully stirring hearing this tune at 4am in a foreign land.

I watch a game show, lots of adverts for shampoo and toothpaste, a French detective show, a dubbed version, in French of Bullseye with Jim Bowen, presumably telling a bespectacled couple from Barnsley "hard lines, come and have a look at what you could have won" whilst a skinny woman in a bikini straddles a motor boat that Jim tells the audience was used in the Rio video for the recent hit by Duran Duran. They didn't half enjoy rubbing the contestants noses in it – when they won it was never a speedboat, more like a Lada classic in chestnut brown.

Andrew Foley Jones

Please Don't Take Me Home - A Cat Called Robson-Kanu

DAY TWO: THE DAY OF THE OPENING GAME.

I wake to the sound of tram brakes that honestly feel like they are passing through our apartment. Strangely the Pringle from beneath the fridge is no longer there; instead there's an Orangina bottle top and a rook from a chess set, his eyes coloured menacingly in blood red. I've either dreamt it, or these household objects have been having a party as I slept.

Richard is snoring like an industrial town. It's like being in a saw mill or factory that makes lintels. I want to so much for this noise to stop. I approach all tentative like a Matador approaching a scary old bull. I have the urge to smother him. I wonder where he's put the match tickets. If I kill him, I might not be able to get in. He moves slightly in his sleep. I don't know why but I fear he may buckaroo like that 1980s board game and send me crashing through the fourth floor window.

I consider my options and decide the best way forward is to poke him in the side like I once saw Steve Irwin jab a bloated python which had a spring lamb stuck in his throat (serves you right Mr Python) and he moves a little. He makes an other-worldly growling sound that prompts me to spray some Lynx Panther over his face. It however does nothing but make the room smell a bit more aromatic. If anything, he's snoring louder. I really want to smother him. If you've ever been confronted with this dilemma, you'll feel my pain – it really is the most frustrating thing ever.

Eventually he stirs, opens his eyelids and says: "Morning, how you getting on - oh what a terrible night's sleep (and)… why does the room smell of Lynx Panther?"

Incredible. I'm going to have to rethink the sleeping arrangements on this trip. I cannot cope with this level of nocturnal sleep pollution. I love you dearly Richard but sort yourself out – sew a golf ball to the back of your pyjamas, have a nose job, please do something if not for me and my sanity but for your good lady wife, Elizabeth.

I decide it would be futile to attempt any more sleep what with the snoring and the trams and feeling that some kitchen debris might come alive and try and strangle me and we agree to get ourselves ready and make our way out and find some breakfast.

I FaceTime Kinsella and he's at home in Ireland and I speak to Valerie, his lovely mum and he tells me to retweet his mornings tweets, the egotist, and he tells me Ireland are going to win the 'whole fecking tournament' and I tell him to go and see his psychologist and he tells me where to go and hangs up, as far as you can hang up on FaceTime.

I tweet something about Wrexham not having enough players to make up a six a side team and this gets 7 retweets and 9 favourites pretty quickly which I'm pleased about and social media is a lot about egos, isn't it? How many retweets, likes, favourites. We all like to be liked. Does it make us feel more successful, liked, appreciated? I'm sure there's someone far cleverer than I doing a PhD on it right now.

I also often wonder whether the success of the team you support, in whichever sporting discipline that's your thing, has any impact on how your life develops. For instance, does success as a spectator encourage a person to be successful or does it create apathy? Does conversely, repetitive loss, mirror your life and make you settle you for defeat or does it spur you on to better yourself in your every day life?

Or does it all really mean fuck all? Anyhow, I'm liking this social media business and I post a fuzzy picture of my match ticket and watch as the retweets, the favourites accumulate - yeah baby, I'm a successful person.

We shower (not together) and dress and descend the 78 steps, consuming 29 calories as we do. A casual stroll along the waterside and then randomly around this lovely city, we get through 267 calories or one and a third croissants, or two fifths of a bottle of Pelforth Brun, (*5) the new beverage of choice that will become like a friend to me over the coming weeks.

Now I should I explain, that this calorie thing, isn't an obsessive disorder of mine; it's just I've got a new app called Endomondo which tracks calories and distances walked and ran. I suppose it does become a bit of an obsession but it's not the worst thing in the world to become obsessed over; it beats heroin or radical fundamentalism I suppose. I once thought about buying one of those Slendertones, the devices you strap to your stomach and they vibrate and give you a six pack – I always liked the idea of doing it whilst eating a massive takeaway: another paradox of sorts.

We find a café and order coffee and croissant and anything else with any stereotypical substance. My French is pretty basic and to be fair, Richard is far superior although I think he makes a little go a long way round.

Sitting at a pavement café drinking wonderful coffee and eating a lovely croissant, watching the city coming alive is an incredible experience and anticipating our opening game in a major tournament is something very special that I will truly never forget.

I Facetime my sister and talk a bit about pride and patriotism and the line between patriotism and nationalism being a thin one and it's something we certainly need to be mindful of. I mean, the earth was not created with borders; we put them in. Patriotism I gather is a good thing whereas nationalism can with the wrong methodology behind it, be a terribly destructive thing.

I catch up on the news back home, lots of political manoeuvring over the EU Referendum, more American shootings, mortgage lending at an all time high since the crash, suicide bombings in Iraq, somebody calling Tony Blair a liar, no more signings by Wrexham, a thread on Red Passion about Danny Ward, our ex goalkeeper, now at Liverpool and there's a rumour that he might be involved in the Slovakia game tonight. I take a look on Twitter and there's nothing there so it can't be true can it? Twitter is after all my go to guy for substantiated news and fact.

We wander around the city and rack up 5kms on the Endomondo app and I take a look at my All Saints shorts on E Bay and the Wrexham football programme from my first ever game. Everything is under control. Bid at the last 5 seconds, that's my strategy.

We meet Alan, a friend and fellow Wrexham supporter who I went to University with, some 25 years ago, when Wales were really shit. Wrexham were actually not as shit and were a division higher than we are now, in League 2. We used to go and watch Wrexham away in an old red mini, visiting exotic places like Scunthorpe and Doncaster and Bury –we may have even been to Rotherham but maybe I'm romanticising.

We've kept in touch but there's something quite surreal about walking into a restaurant in France about to watch Wales in a major tournament and seeing him sat there in his George Berry t shirt. He's been going to away games with Wales for years whilst I've been to most home games over the past thirty years, he definitely falls within the category of a Superfan and super fans don't wear replica shirts; they wear quirky bespoke merchandise.

Alan has accrued a group of 47 for the meal, consisting of various individuals from different groups of people met over his life. We quickly make new acquaintances who, unknown to us at that moment as we tuck into our sea bass and beetroot jus, will become integral components to our summer adventure in France. The restaurant was on Rick Steins Long Weekend TV show not so long ago and fair play to the fish restauranteur this is a decent place.

Towards the end of the meal, the realisation sinks in that there's still four hours to negotiate; that's four hours of drinking and singing time. There's a real danger I'll be paralytic by kick off. There have been I confess, some black spots during my spectating history - II remember a game once in Blackpool where I don't remember anything apart from a hail storm – we by all accounts lost 4-1 or 4-0 that day – and then there was Port Vale in the FA Cup where I'm sure I saw Robbie Williams dropping a jumbo hot dog and everybody sang 'Let Me Entertain You' to him as he tried to wipe of some mustard and fried onions from his replica top. There's a chance I dreamt that one up but you get the idea: I can't miss the opening game. I'll have to devise a fool proof water tight plan to stay in the game.

THE OPENING GAME - SLOVAKIA IN BORDEAUX

My plan goes something like this: I ask the waiter for a dark beer – Pelforth Brun perhaps? He shrugs like only French waiters can and tells me they do not deal with Pelforth as they only allow seven days credit. He does one of those French shrugs indicating that brewery can go fuck themselves and ask if he deals with any other dark ale proprietors who maybe offer slightly more favourable credit lines at which he smiles, walks away and returns some thirty seconds later with a tall thin glass which looks like it has been dipped into a pot of molasses (*6).

I sip the concoction; it tastes like tar, strong very alcoholic tar. It's a challenge to force it down my neck. I ask him what percentage it is. He holds up his entire set of fingers and two thumbs before closing his fist and holding another two fingers into the air. On standing up and inspecting the pump, he means that it's 10.2% proof. It's not the gentle beverage I had envisaged would lead me up to kick off time. I'm going to be well pissed if I crack on with that.

Exuberant alcohol proof aside, this is a really lovely place and the waiter shows us the menu on a rustic old blackboard and we order and the food is fantastic and we talk about Welshness and I admit that sometimes, not being a fluent Welsh speaker can be difficult and you can sometimes feel a little less Welsh when surrounded by Welsh speakers.

Living in a North Wales resort town meant people would come on holiday, often like it more than the industrial town they had come from and then decided they wanted to migrate there. There's absolutely nothing wrong with that. Even your average Brexiteer can't argue with such behaviour. However, from a cultural perspective, it can cause problems: dilution, evaporation, whatever you want to call it - the indigenous population to an extent will become a smaller ratio, year on year and so with it, matters that were particular to that location will shift, such as speaking the mother tongue.

The population of Prestatyn was about 20,000 as I grew up in the 1970s and as it increased, the proportion of immigrants for want of a better word transcended into every crevice of town life. Walking down the high street the beautiful melody of the Welsh language that I would frequently hear as a small child, walking to the Chapel with my Naini who used to play the organ there became less and less – a little like the chirrup of a rare bird slowly being decimated until there aren't many left at all.

In those days, I would understand Welsh and be able to speak it, my grandparents and their generation would only speak Welsh, at home, in the corner shop, in Chapel. Suddenly, you would notice English dialects creeping into the locality. Manchester, Liverpool, Stoke typically and with it, you'd hear less Welsh and in school, significantly, it became less cool to speak Welsh.

It doesn't however erode your feeling of Welshness: you still love being Welsh more than anything else. You just don't sound as Welsh, and particularly in situations like this, you do sometimes feel a little bit of an imposter.
On Twitter I receive confirmation that Danny Ward will be

making his debut; Wayne Hennessey, the first choice goalkeeper is injured and the rookie keeper is going to start. It's great news for Wrexham FC as it triggers a bonus payment negotiated when he was transferred to Liverpool. But you can't help but think it could be bad news for Wales with someone so inexperienced being drafted in for such a historic game.

I manage to consume a few glasses of the strong ale, coupled with a couple of red wine chasers but I've kept it together and as we leave the restaurant whilst admittedly a little wobbly, I have been much worse. It's been a truly magical meal. Rick Stein we salute you.

We clamber onto a tram assuring ourselves that this is the right way to the stadium. The problem seems to be that nobody has actually checked the official map and everybody just seems to be following anybody else dressed in red. We could be heading in completely the opposite direction.

The tram stops suddenly and after two or three minutes of dazed confusion, we all alight and work our way towards an engineering structure that is either a very large multi-storey car park or an international football stadium. Luckily, it is the latter and as we approach the steps leading to the arena, a surge of pure football spectating adrenaline soars through our alcohol filled veins.

I won't go into too much detail about the game itself as this has been well documented save that it would be amiss for me not to mention the feelings that I have never experienced at a sporting event when the anthem was played. It is always something that I'm sure for any Welsh person is a song that makes you tingle but never before have I felt so proud and felt such an affinity to my great country. Yes, there's a fine line between Nationalism and Patriotism and this is definitely on the right side of it.

We were watching from a neutral zone (which happened to be the case in all of our games as we missed out on the ballot to sit with the hard core Welsh support) and I happen to be filming the moment when Gareth Bale scored our first goal in the trademark free kick whilst Hal Robson-Kanu's scuffed winner sent us into raptures. It's truly one of my footballing highlights and at the end of the game, I really don't want to leave the stadium. It's a strange emotion when you feel such euphoria at a sporting event: I wonder if this is heightened when you aren't used to such success – surely it must diminish if you support a team that wins more often than not?

We stay for a while and sing and watch the wonderful spectacle of the children of the Welsh players coming out onto the pitch and dribbling the ball into the net in front of where the majority of the Welsh fans are assembled. Each goal is cheered as much as Robson- Kanu's winner and it's a fitting end to an incredibly patriotic occasion, an apt tribute to the feeling of family and community that being out there, part of a large group of like minded people and those back home, can only generate.

After reluctantly leaving the stadium, Face Timing everyone I could think of, we jump on a tram and head back into the centre of town where we happen upon a glorious pub called The Apollo. I order a celebratory bottle of red from a local vineyard and we talk about the day, the game, chat to some Hungarians who ask are we going to leave the EU to which I reply, I wouldn't think so.

We play a frame of pool that I lose badly and I blame the wine and the euphoria and adrenalin that is surging through me. We head outside and sit with the locals and through the window we see that England have gone one nil up which is disappointing but it doesn't really impact on my feeling of complete ecstasy. Then just to make the day even more special, Russia score a last minute equalizer and if Carlsberg did perfect days, then this might just be it.

We reluctantly leave the Apollo and venture towards the main square and drink with some Hungarians and Slovakians, teaching them the lyrics to "Don't take me home" and the rather mono syllabic "Hal Robson-Kanu" leaving just the melody of the national anthem rather than trying to teach them the actual words.

There's absolutely no hint of any violence at all whilst in the background on television screens in all of the bars, images of England and Russian fans fighting in the stadium and in the streets from tonight's game flash eerily as if being transmitted from a different planet.

We wander around a few more bars and everywhere, Welsh songs swirl around the French night and different nationalities share anecdotes, souvenirs, I even witness some shirt swapping – it was all incredibly good natured. I don't remember getting home but I wake in the morning on the kitchen floor having somehow negotiated the now notorious 78 steps up to our apartment. It is rumoured that I ascended with the assistance of a piggy back administered by Richard but until I receive any photographic verification, this tale remains firmly in the folder labelled 'Hearsay or Urban Myth.'

We spend the next day wandering around town, having a few pints, reminiscing about yesterday's events, Richard still trying to claim he piggy backed me up the steps. He may even have put something on Facebook about it. The red wine hangover hinders me not and I'm absolutely loving the aftermath of our victory.

On the Monday, we board our flight from Bordeaux to Paris and just before take off are sent an email from Air France saying that the onward flight to Manchester has been cancelled due to a pilot strike. We quickly book an Airbnb for 3 nights in Paris and several conversations with SFJ attempt to solve the quandary regarding our match tickets which are somewhere in Richard's office.

After much faff we decide to try and get home and upon landing in Paris, we manage to book another flight to Liverpool for which we are grateful as another three alcohol fuelled days in Paris is not really what we need right now. We need to get home and have some work and recuperation ready for the big game with England taking place on Thursday. And, let's be honest, we couldn't guarantee getting the tickets across in readiness for the next game.

We manage to get the flight and we return home and the

next couple of days are uneventful – we go to work, we wash our clothes and book a flight to Belgium with an onward train on to Lens where the game is being staged. We unfortunately cannot get a flight back in time so will have to get a coach/ferry/coach combination straight back after the game.

Andrew Foley Jones

AS LONG AS WE BEAT THE ENGLISH, I DON'T CARE: THE STEREOPHONICS

Some might see this ideology as a tad sad, a touch bitter, an enormous geographical chip on our Taf Shoulders. Who knows, maybe we have.

The day went like this:

As we approach the French border and change trains, the first feel of potential trouble hits us with a large presence of England fans on the platform being herded around by heavily armed French police. Whilst there are many Welsh fans at present at the train station, we are far outnumbered by the English followers dressed in various versions of their shitty white replica jersey.

The town and all surrounding network links to it, have been designated an alcohol free zone in an attempt to avert a potential flashpoint and on the train, police confiscate several Fanta and Pepsi bottles which don't contain the liquid for which they were intended.
One man, who sounds like he might be from Port Vale or Wolverhampton offers me a swig from a can of diet Irn Bru that I think might possibly be piss.

No thanks mucker.

As we approach the stadium, it soon transpires that alcohol is being sold in the city centre and there is a strangely carnival atmosphere in the streets with groups of Welsh and English drinking in the same bars. It's isn't the Armageddon we had anticipated. I wish I hadn't bothered with the stab proof vest.

We find the bar which the coach company, Gullivers, have seconded for the afternoon, collect our tickets and are told where the buses will meet after the game and have some pre-match beverages. Got to say, the thought of a drive back through the night doesn't fill me with glee and I suppose the result will have a large part to play in the pleasure of our return.

I'm trying to meet my mates Andrew and Jacqui De Looze who own a great little coffee shop in Chester called Baristas on Watergate Street but there's absolutely no signal on my phone and the airwaves are clearly jammed with the thousands who have descended on the city.

The place we've assembled at is effectively a night club. Despite it being early afternoon it's pitch black in here, illuminated by flashing neon, glitterballs and the like. To add to the weirdness, there's communal pizza doing the rounds and I'm tasked with going round the tables, collecting left over slices of pepperoni, having a bit of an issue with a character from Newport who enters into some type of tug of war with a full margarita I found on the edge of the dance floor. I try and explain over the din of The Manics Motorcycle Emptiness that there's going to be no winners in all this and let's just split it but he's having none of it and inevitably the pizza splits, the covering flopping to the floor like Robbie Savage's pre quiff curtains.

We bump into a couple of lads from Prestatyn and we hug and drink more beer and hug and drink more beer and I'm sent on another mission to find some hot dogs that are rumoured to be doing the rounds. It turns out to be a myth I'm sure and all I find is a bowl of ready salted hula hoops and I eat these, from my fingers as of course you are supposed to do.

I am becoming anxious. I so much want to win this game.

As the kick off time approaches, we wander around the streets and attempt to find our section, on the way bumping into former Wales and Wrexham and Wigan centre forward, Neil Roberts, decked very cooly in the actual shirt he wore during one of his caps for his country. How cool is that.

We make our way to the stadium where we are again sat in a "neutral zone." It soon transpires however that we are very much in the minority and as the ground fills up, the main stand where we are sat, must be 99% English.

Richard considers that we perhaps should not celebrate in the unlikely event that we have any success but as the anthem begins, we are both up on our feet belting out the words, ignoring the occasional choice verbal abuse being metaphorically pelted at us.

I am really not expecting to get anything from the game although out of all the matches this is the one I would love to win the most.

We however start off poorly and to be fair are almost overran. I fear the worse. It could be a tonking. It really could. We repel wave after wave of attack and are then awarded a soft freekick what seems a lifetime out from the England goal - some respite from the onslaught at last.

You wouldn't believe what happened next - well you would, as you've probably all seen it some time ago - yes, the magician himself - Gareth Bale steps up and Joe Hart only happens to fluff the ball into the corner of his own net: our celebrations are exuberant and we really don't care about the risk of violence which becomes more and more tangible and apparent as half time arrives and Wales are in an unexpected 1-0 lead. I don't think I've ever been pumped as much from a goal in my life.

Whilst I've been to hundreds of football matches during my life and have been in several sticky situations, there is often "football banter" that takes place which doesn't make you fear for your safety. During this game, many of the comments and the body language of the English fans was way more than banter and some of the stereotypical nonsense that came from their mouths was truly appalling. On the one hand, it was frightening to think that somebody could actually think these things but to actually think it is socially acceptable to say them out loud is something altogether more amazing.

When the equalizer went in the atmosphere improved and by the time the injury time winner was knocked in by Daniel Sturridge, we were well on our way through the exits on our way to the sanctuary of our coach and the onwards journey via a ferry from Calais to Dover and the long road journey through the night back to Wrexham and a taxi to Chester.

Andrew Foley Jones

That has to be one of the worst football matches I have ever attended both in terms of the fear factor and the result but once I was on the ferry after a couple of hours contemplation staring into the English channel, the disappointment soon subsided replaced with pride and a realisation that we are a small nation, sat amongst the English hoards today, despite defeat, never have I ever felt prouder to be a Welshman: the ability to take defeat with grace is an important as it is to win with dignity and respect: and we only need a point to get through so onward to Toulouse.

But you know what, if things hadn't worked out as they eventually did, this would be been one hard fucking pill to swallow. I won't go too much into it, as in isolation it was in any way you want to dress it up, a bad smudge of lipstick on an enormously ugly and viscous pig.

It was an awful day, long (every type of transport know to man), vitriolic, involved a ferry and a coach home and at every stage I was sandwiched in by horrible smug, arrogant English. If I didn't know what was going to happen it would have been a dark day.

I think however I kind of predicted it was a mere blip, a bump in the road, when I, took stock and sought solace in the grey choppy waters of the English Channel after a mind numbing and reality checking visual of the huge refugee camp on the outskirts of Calais that made you count your poultry and not to be disappointed at the woeful mess of your life story based on an injury time winner by the awful Daniel Sturridge.

This is a fixture I was both dreading and looking forward to in equal measure. The fear I suppose I getting a real Royal tonking from the old enemy, a real thrashing that will have Alan Shearer and Ian Wright and other sanctimonious toss pots salivating into their bangers and mash.

People question why we detest the English so much, limited you'll understand to sporting events. It is perhaps something that you are born into, a feeling that comes from the heart and the soul and which stays with you, intense until the day you die.

I have friends who have migrated to Wales as adolescents and who now class themselves very much as Welsh but who will willingly without duress of say a revolver to the temple, or an electric probe strapped above their bath support England.

They are missing, perhaps through not being born within the principality that inherent feeling of Welshness that brings with it an inherent disliking (loathing) of our cousins from across the Dyke.

Now listen, this is not a book of History, and I never once profess to be an expert in such things - but nevertheless, it is something that is hugely relevant to the psyche of being Welsh.

We all know what happened, it was our only loss but to see those bewildered faces as Joe Hart soap squirmed the ball into his net from a Bale free kick was worth with hindsight the pain of defeat. Ever since he did those 'Head and Shoulders' adverts he was asking for trouble.

"Soap in his eyes."

"Like a bottle of shampoo."

He was just asking for it.

The verbal onslaught from those dressed in the white and red of the old enemy was pretty intense and intimidating.

"Top knot wanker."

"Coal sucking cunts."

And my particular favourite.

"Sheep fucking retards."

All rained down from the collective hoards.

The only experience of English Wales games in the past included a 4-1 win in the now defunct Home Internationals which I remember hearing on the radio as I played football with David Williams in my garden, God rest his soul. My dad was at that game with Mike England in charge.

Comically, the next time we had any form of interaction with Mr England was when he had to give, in a wholly deserved and respectful manner, I must add, our family a collective bollocking for my Taid's behaviour whilst a guest at his Rhyl based nursing Home.

My mum's father, always a bit of a character, was a little

flirtatious with the nursing staff shall we say. This gave way to a yellow card. You couldn't really complain. A second yellow soon followed after an incident with an unauthorised drinking session in the Swan Public House which culminated in an incident involving a head on with an electric wheelchair – rumour had it he had escaped, got pissed and collided with a mobility scooter or the like. Even Mark Clattenburg would have struggled to have let him off. It was if anything a straight red. Way to go Taid – you went out in style, I'll give you that.

I must confess to having some admiration for this type of behaviour as you approach the end of your time and sure enough, after his expulsion, to a home in Prestatyn, he soon passed away.

Anyhow, that victory was perhaps one of the reasons why the once hugely popular (amongst the Scots, Irish, Nor Irish and us Welsh at least) tournament got kicked into touch. I think football related violence got the blame but I think the reality was 'England really didn't like it up 'em Mr Mannering.' So it got booted into touch and we only got to play the Mighty English if we were unfortunate enough to draw them in the Qualification stages for the Euros or the World Cup. The only other time I indeed were to witness such a battle in person was when I watched a Mark Hughes side lose (as we often did then) tamely at Old Trafford 2-0 with a Millwall fan deciding it would be of added comfort if I were to watch the game with his knee rested in the nape of my back. I doubt it will ever take off in places like airplanes and cinema seats. Telling me he was going to knife me at full time was another added pleasure of playing England and is perhaps another added sub text into my disconnection with them as a people, a race, a sporting opponent.

And it I suppose, lies both ways. In Chester, where I have chosen to live (hypercritically deciding to live in England when there is all that land and space in my beloved Wales to chose from - perhaps) there is a fervent anti Welsh feeling.

One only has to tag onto to the daily walking tour amidst the Japanese, the Koreans, the Americans, Canadians, Italians and Spanish and hear the story of why the Chester Town Hall clock only has three sides and that the reason why the side facing east towards the principality of Wales does not is because "... the English choose not to give the Welsh the time of day" which always brings a ripple of laughter from these visiting tourists and a sigh from myself on the days where I tag on, if perhaps only to give myself an added reminder of why the English are collectively deemed as cocks in the most general sense possible. The fair accomplice is the rule that apparently after dusk, a Welsh man (nee person) can be shot and killed by a perpetrator carrying as you do a cross bow without any penalty or retribution in the realms of justice whatsoever.

At this, I mention to the guide, typically an overweight man dressed as a Roman so keen as to signify the proud Roman roots of the city(no xylophonic feelings towards Italians) and expose this for the tourist urban myth that it is and maybe it is my pedantic legal training that tends me towards the declaration to all that the common law offence of murder would, of course override any such historic bye law and that really, should we allow a little fact to get in the way of fiction, as I wave farewell and walk off clockwise around the glorious Roman Walls in the direction of Wales and Home.

So yes, I have chosen to live in England and if this makes me a hypocrite then hold me down and shoot me in the face with a cross bow.

There are lots of lovely English people out there by the way. Borders are of course man made. But in sporting terms, Christ you've got a bigger proportion that most, of real wankers out there. I've seen them and to the ones who went to shake my hand after the game only to pull away their hands at the last minute and give me a close up wanker sign right in my face, hope you really enjoyed the Iceland game. I really did.

#Forever stronger.

I post these words on Facebook and Twitter and as we board the coach back home, I feel the excitement building again in readiness for the group decider against Russia in Toulouse on Monday 20th June 2016.

Andrew Foley Jones

CARCASSONE AND THEN ONTO THE ACTION IN TOULOUSE

Richard has been here before. We decided it would be nice to head off the beaten track for a day or so before heading over to Toulouse for the big group decider. And he's quite right, it's a stunning place and if you haven't been and fancy a bit of romancing, you could do far worse.

We have one of the nicest meals in our life and in reality, there should be some real romancing going on here, not two football fans, dressed in the best clothes they could fit into an undersized piece of hand luggage.

Alan and his party rather belatedly find the place whilst we're half way through our main. A girl called (name removed for legal reasons: oh go on then, Gillian) who we met in Bordeaux, comically walking in up the steps in her southern west Wales twang declaring she was "fucking knackered" as she walked into the room full of diners. I had only wished she was wearing her retro 1976 kit that she had on when we had last met to add another dollop of comedy to the already hilarious scenario. Sorry Gillian, now I know you live in That London and all that and have a fancy job in The City but you can't take the girl out of Cardigan and all that.

We head around the corner for a late pint and watch the end of another match and start listening in to a conversation on another table which goes something like this:

"Rotten shark tastes very much as if you could dream to imagine. You've got to do it right - you're in a big oblong room with your work peers and everyone's doing it and although it really tastes like animal shit or a kangaroo cock, you're chewing it down, whacking it back with some equally foul tasting spirit that you knock back like your sorry suck ass life depends on it" says a man who looks like he's lived a life.

The other man, obviously a German says-

"Do you have to be so fucking stereotypical: you'll be humming a Bjork song before we know it."

It's quite funny for a German and the other man starts to laugh, clicking his glass against that of the German and necking the shot that was in it, hailing another set for him and the German and it seems, anyone else in their vicinity.

"But I do really," he chuckles, his voice all gravel and volcano ash "fucking love nothing more than a rotten shark sandwich whilst listening to the greatest fucking hits of Sigur Ros (*8)" he says, howling now chinking his glass against that of a Hungarian who turn chinks glasses with a Slovak.

It's like the United fucking Nations in here but without the Americans trying to invade everything. We start chatting and it turns out he's from Iceland, who, alongside Wales, appear to the darlings so far of the tournament.

I ask what he does.

A fisherman he says. I specialise in squid he adds.

He smiles and hands me a shot glass.

Drink he urges.

The Hungarian and the Slovac and the German all gesture for me to drink and as I neck it, another glass is handed to me, the process repeated several times.

After the chaos of the first few days of the tournament this seems a completely different planet. The ugly scenes on the streets of Marseille where English fans invaded with a hostility and lack of respect that seems to be embedded in their psyche, a legacy perhaps of centuries of invasion, empire, exploration and overstated self importance.

As I sit and watch this scene unfold, I wonder, probably half pissed, is a cross section of football spectators a microcosm, a petri dish of a country's social economic behaviour.

The video footage, the pictures in the press, on social media, our experience in Lens all points to an ugly indictment to what has been referred to previously as 'the English Disease.'

I head through the streets of Carcassonne, stopping on the way in a souvenir shop to have the mandatory photograph of me in a warriors hat and sword; my post of Facebook attracting an impressive number of likes.

I've never been really interested in Facebook but this liking business could become quite addictive. Is this the only reason people use it? It must be conversely pretty dispiriting where you have only single digits likes. My uncle I notice, who I have befriended during this trip, likes and shares his own posts. I'm unsure as to the etiquette but this show doesn't feel right. Anyhow, each to their own.

I try and track down Alan as we head towards home but there's no signal; whilst I really wanted a night cap with him and his mad cap crew, there's something in the chaos of modern society, cathartic about not being able to reach people, to not be reached: sometimes you can't but help that there is not enough space and peace in life.

Mobiles are amazing but there's also that fear and dread that appears to accompany its ownership. It's like we have to have them on us at all time. I picture the evolutionary diagram depicted by Darwin as ape passed to Neanderthal to modern day man, will soon have a new prototype where the human being has a third limb in the guise of a smart phone growing out of the dominant hand.

Yes mobile phones are amazing but our reliance and the lack of social awareness that follows from their usage is surely having an enormous impact of the way in which we interact and behave as a social group.

We return to our Airbnb and I hastily arrange my disposable bedsheets left in a plastic pouch at the base of my bed and try to sleep before Richard commences his snoring. It works as I sleep incredibly well and wake refreshed and ready for the decisive game against the might of Russia.

As I clean my teeth, stealing some of Richards Aquafresh (the one with the three stripes), I recall a European qualifying second leg play off defeat in Cardiff some years ago and remember clearly a group of Russians taunting me after the game.

It's funny how things like that stay in your head. I wonder if, twenty years on, the same people are here now, feeling the same surge of nervous anticipation that I, as I swig on another fine cup of coffee looking over an intersection in the centre of Carcassonne, feel, realising that I really am what can only be described as completely immersed in this experience: as sporting pursuits go, this really is something else.

We travel by train to Toulouse and after dumping off our meagre travel baggage we head into the square and embark on a wonderful afternoon drinking with fellow Welsh and Russians. We swap anecdotes and flags and take photographs and a friendly bar man charges my I phone as I drink Pelforth Brun and gather my thoughts for the big night.

RUSSIA: THE GROUP DECIDER

Before the game, in the stadium, I borrow a traditional Russian hat off a woman who is sat behind me. I post this on Facebook and Michael O'Kane instantly puts on a comment and a photo showing the woman I took the hat from, frozen on a TV image from the coverage he is watching from back home. A camera man, whilst scanning the crowd, typically for decent looking women, has focused in on her and O'Kane has captured the moment.

She's surrounded by a group of very tough Russian men; perhaps she is a famous actress, or the wife of a Gang Lord. The cameraman has picked her out rather than myself which is fine; and on a wider level I'm amazed the world of political correctness hasn't stopped this practise that indeed takes place at every international football tournament. Argentinians are my favourites, if you were asking.

Anyhow I have bigger fish to fry and we settle down for the game of our lives. It turns out there was no need for nerves as Wales completely dominate the game. A two nil lead soon makes this a far more comfortable victory than you could ever imagine. A third is almost unthinkable but it arrives and it really could have been more.

I look around the stadium and imagine whose who taunted me in Cardiff all those years ago and think of the social and economic changes these people have seen over their life time.

I turn round to see the hat woman leaving the ground

together with lots of other Russians whose time in France is prematurely at an end. I recall the play off loss so many years ago and feel a certain emotion of vengeance which sounds negative and it isn't meant to. A kind of sporting retribution is perhaps a better way of putting it.

Someone on Facebook has posted, having seen her on the TV that she is after all a famous Russian model, hence the group of rather large Russian men in her vicinity.

We hang around the stadium again and watch the children coming out to do the now traditional post match kick around. A goal by Gareth Bales daughter creates the biggest cheer of the night. Later in the tournament UEFA in their twisted glory declare that this behaviour isn't allowed under their rules – whereas widespread corruption is – work that one out. They also in time during the subsequent World Cup qualifying campaign charge us and Northern Ireland with our supporters wearing poppy images which also falls foul of their rules. UEFA and FIFA need sorting, root and branch style.

We leave the stadium, take a wrong turn, take two hours to reach the city centre, getting lost down dead ends, passing groups of Russians who despite looking rather menacing, don't attack us with metal rods, which is a massive bonus and despite everywhere being closed, we find a drink and a kebab and celebrate our progression from the group stages.

To compound our euphoria, England have been held to a nil nil draw to Slovakia meaning that we have finished top of our group. Who'd have Adam and Eve'd it, as Andrew Kinsella would say, in his new cockney twang.

Please Don't Take Me Home - A Cat Called Robson-Kanu

We've made it through the group stages.

We're staying in France.

Who'd have thought it.

Please don't take me home.

I think in all seriousness, ridiculous as it sounds, of the cat in the cage jeering at me.

I hope you're watching Mr Cat is sadly all I can think at this most wondrous of times.

Andrew Foley Jones

THE NIGHT BEFORE BREXIT

We've returned home for some much needed recuperation and I go for an early evening run around the Walls in Chester passing by the hoards of tourists that the city attracts. It's a truly beautiful city and if you haven't visited, you should give it a go.

I return home and look forward to settling down to the Italy V Ireland game, a match which Ireland must win to have any chance to progress in the tournament. I class Ireland as my second team, not only because of my father's Irish roots – with the name Foley being his original surname before his parents tragically died when he was a baby leaving him to be adopted by a distant Welsh relative called Jones - but we had viewed the masses of Irish supporters in France with a feeling of genuine Celtic kinship and a wonderful stereotypical comradery which they bring with them to any sporting or indeed other cultural events that they are part of. If the people are a good barometer of a nation, then the Irish always enhance their national brand wherever they travel.

Just as I am showering away the grime and sweat of my 5 km run, I answer a Facetime call from Richard who whilst admittedly surprised as to my state of undress in the shower, tells me I should drop by to a bar and deli situated in Chester just a few hundred metres from where we live. To protest would be futile so I confirm I will wander down after I have showered and dried myself. In the condensation on the shower wall, I subliminally consider that I have been writing "Cymru Am Byth" in the condensation that has been formed by the scoldingly hot water that I love to shower to after finishing a run. I dry myself and resist putting on my Welsh replica jersey and instead put on a pair of tailored shorts and a new All Saints t-shirt and wander over.

When I arrive, I note there are a number of our friends already sitting around an inside table swigging on various tumblers containing a clear liquid that turns out to be gin; I have inadvertently walked into a gin tasting evening. I've got to say, I've walked into worst things – walls, fists, the upturned studs of Michael O'Kane.

I am two behind and dispense with these quickly and nod in agreement whilst a gentleman well versed in all things gin related, tells me that the third glass I am about to consume is "brewed" (is gin brewed?) in a distant farmhouse in the Scottish Highlands. It has a bouquet of thistle and heather he puts forward and I nod, somehow muttering the words "thistle and heather, yes, thistle and heather" whilst all around me nod their heads in agreement and to be honest it just tastes exactly the same as the last two tumblers of gin that now sit in the base of my wary stomach.

Nevertheless, never wanting to be shy of trying to learn new skills, regardless of my scepticism, I join in the consumption of another three or five tumblers of gin each housing a different type of herb or fruit. On the penultimate glass, I find myself saying "herbaceous" when the gentleman asks what we the gin drinking public think of this latest concoction. He nods and says over and over "yes, herbaceous" nodding again (and) "you can taste the thyme and the parsley with subtle overtones of oak and truffle."

I genuinely haven't got a clue what this bloke is going on about but I nod likely a crazy mad dog, nodding for a bone from the local crazy butcher, who dangles it in front of you in the sky like the tablet for eternal youth.

I wash the gin down with a pint of Cheshire Cat and then nibble on some snacks that have somehow appeared in the centre of our table. I notice it's past 11 and I have missed the Italy Ireland game. My plans for a quiet night in have been dashed and sadly I am yet again, inebriated. I need to go to sleep. I need to make sure all of my replica football shirts are clean and dry and ready for the next stage of this epic adventure.

As we consider our departure, somebody begins to debate upon the pending referendum. They say don't discuss religion or politics and this is one of the reasons why we should always in a social setting amongst friends, resist from asking how somebody is going to vote. It's a social stigma for a reason. People, just don't go there.

I decide it would be prudent to mine sweep the last embers of gin scattered about the thick oak table. I notice a clear chasm soon appears through the centre of the table between those who are going to vote IN and those who are going to vote OUT: I am surprised at those who said they would vote out and even more concerned by the seemingly lack of information their decision has been founded upon.

I have no problem with people having different electoral or political views to make – all I ask is that any vote is given with some forethought and some properly considered knowledge. It appears that many of the decisions have turned on some basic tabloid propaganda revolving around immigration and the cost of membership of the EU and its proposed reinvestment into the National Health Service.

Anyhow, the debate is good natured and we all exit for home, heavy on gin and the pending last 16 match against Northern Ireland in Paris in a couple of days time and to a far lesser extent, the excitement that always surrounds a vote of any kind. We meander through the pretty streets of Chester and return home and as I slip into a dreamy sleep, never would I imagine that tomorrow's vote would go the way it did.

THE DAY OF THE REFERENDUM

I put another decent fourteen hour shift in and then on my way home meet Andrew Kinsella and we together with SFJ go to the HQ building in Chester to register our respective votes.

We are all openly voting "Remain" and amongst the idle chit chat outside the voting booths and the anecdotal information flashing around social media, it feels as predictable as Wrexham setting up with a lone striker in a dire 4-5-1 formation; there is a feeling of certainty that this is the way the vote will go.

We return home and watch the initial results coming through and soon realise it is not going to be as cut and dry as we first anticipated. Still, an EXIT vote is inexplicable. I stay up and in my dozy state, start to realise the unthinkable is going to happen and when I wake shortly after 4.30am, David Dimbleby declares the unbelievable breaking news that the UK is leaving the European Union.

There is a feeling of despair and destruction in the air; social media is awash with different viewpoints, some gloating as to the incredibly victory whilst others share both their disappointment and distain at those who have voted to leave. The country appears to have a huge chasm going through it.

My initial fear is that this is a protest vote gone way too far based on propaganda fed to us by a charismatic and enigmatic "leave" campaign whereas the "remainers" appear to have been a little lethargic and apathetic, contributing to this result.

As it turns out over the coming days, the propaganda propounded by the leave campaign is blown out of the water and the subsequent press conferences of amongst others, Boris Johnson, Michael Gove and Nigel Farage appear to show that these protagonists have bitten off more than they can chew leaving an almighty mess to be cleaned up.

As I pack my bag for the trip to Paris on the evening of the referendum decision, I decide I must put this to the back of my mind as otherwise the news will only diminish tomorrow's events in Paris which must be savoured as such days may never come around in my lifetime again.

As we drive down to Folkestone for an overnight stay prior to catching the first tunnel of the day, talk of Brexit is completely off the agenda; perhaps the fear each of the cars inhabitants does not quite trust what the other voted and does not want to find the answer by asking the question.

We arrive fatigued at around 2am and with some hilarity, Richard has booked me in as Lord Bilky of Bulkiness. The check in lady is quickly joined by a cockney gentlemen where they question whether I am really a real life Lord. I reply in the affirmative and they ask why I aren't travelling by private jet or helicopter. I say in Benny Hill style, that I have a massive chopper back on the estate but that I'd rather travel with the ordinary people when going to a football match.

I catch an uneventful three hours sleep in Folkestone and realise upon waking, that whilst concentrating on packing my Welsh memorabilia: 2 large flags, 2 French berets with the Welsh dragon embroidered upon the front, 3 replica shirts, my lucky jeans, I have omitted to include any underwear. A quick text message across the corridor to Richard results in a well ironed pair of Calvin Kleins being slotted under the door – chwarae teg to Richard - you are a good man - and who would have thought these would turn out to be my new lucky underpants

My first trip through the channel tunnel is pretty exciting: as we stand outside the car as we hurtle beneath the channel we mingle with other Welsh and Northern Irish fans and exchange anecdotes and sing songs and generally look forward to the carnival atmosphere that Paris will undoubtedly be filled with over the coming hours. We've also brought with us, I should add SFJ and Elizabeth so they can sample part of our adventure.

We reach our hotel at Charles de Gaulle airport and after marvelling at the iPad controlled TV, radio, music, blinds and even colour scheme in the bathroom, I decide to have a shower to the background of the colour purple and then put on my clothes for the day ahead. I choose my Wales "away" kit but also carry the "home" red shirt which I will then be able to slip on for the game itself to help with making the stadium as red as possible.

We get on a train to central Paris, have some lunch and stumble upon a bar where we are met with the first element of hostility since the England game in Lens, a number of

Please Don't Take Me Home - A Cat Called Robson-Kanu

Northern Irish fans (who are all incidentally clearly from London and are 4th or 5th generation Northern Ireland) and are catching the gravy train now England have been knocked out he tournament, show their disdain as to why Wales as a nation voted for the UK to leave the EU. Attempting to remain calm and not inflame the situation, I explained that we in fact voted remain and that they cannot judge a country by a vote. This calms the situation slightly but nevertheless reveals a perception of what the Brexit means throughout Europe.

I notice the headline and a photograph on the leading French newspaper Le Figaro showing that comical photograph of Boris Johnson tangled up in a zip wire with some headline glibly mocking the UK and its decision to go it alone.

There was a tangible feeling hanging in the air that we are arrogant, unwelcoming and non-inclusive and beyond this, an even more cynical feeling of racism, right winged ideologies and a return to days that we thought were well resigned to the garbage bins of history. With hindsight, I wish I had designed a badge with an EU flag on it saying "I voted remain".

We finish our drinks and I can't help but feel slightly awkward as I make my way through the beautiful streets of Paris and through the Metro, stopping off at the Eiffel Tower to have selfie's of us draped in our wonderful Welsh flag, mingling with the Northern Ireland fans, counting down to the big kick off. I need to put this Brexit thing to the back of my mind; there's a massive football match to deal with.

WALES V NORTHERN IRELAND: THE LAST 16

We outnumber the Northern Ireland fans by some distance and the atmosphere is far more tense than the group stage games. There is a tangible feeling not experienced before that we are not the underdogs anymore; we are expected to win. This is something that doesn't sit pretty with anybody from the principality and certainly not a Wrexham fan.

The first half as expected is to incredibly dour not to, a quality of football that I have domestically become unfortunately accustomed to. Northern Ireland are quite content to make the game into a battle, denying space to the playmakers such as Bale and Ramsay. At half time I cannot help but fear the worse and it is by some distance, the most tense I have been during the whole tournament.

The second half begins the same way although Wales do seem to have stepped up the pace of the game somewhat. A moment of class between Ramsay and Bale culminates in a beautiful cross that is turned into his own net by a Northern Ireland defender and this thankfully proves to be the difference between the two teams.

We are in the quarter finals of the European Championships 2016. I need to write it down again; rent one of those planes that you used to see above Rhyl Beach advertising the Fun Fair and 'It's Brill in Rhyl' on a flag trailing behind it for it to really sink in.

We are in the Quarter Finals of the European Championships 2016.

WE ARE IN THE QUARTER FINALS OF THE EUROPEAN CHAMPIONSHIPS 2016.

We are in the Quarter Finals of the European Championships 2016.

Say it over and over; this is really happening. It all feels rather surreal; it really feels that this isn't happening.

We dive into the first bar outside the stadium where we order perhaps the most expensive round of drinks that's ever been ordered not helped perhaps by the fact that I decide to have a bottle of red wine to myself. Let's face it, if I can't celebrate now, when can I?

We get talking to a German photographer who has just been at the game. He asks if he can take a close up photograph of the crest on my Wales replica kit and I gladly accept and as he edits the result, he tells me that this is his favourite badge in all of international football. He says it depicts strength and unity and is part of why he loves Wales so much. The photo is at the front of the book, just before the introduction - copyright to this anonymous gentleman - thank you.

I can't help but feel immensely proud and realise that this goes way beyond football; the way in which the football team have performed on the pitch and the way the supporters have reacted off it, has produced unprecedented and priceless marketing for Brand Wales that no Wales Tourist Board advertising campaign could even get near.

Andrew Foley Jones

As I look out over an ocean of red shirts filling the streets around the football stadium I feel the clichéd tears of joy and euphoria and pride streaming down my face as the anthem drifts rhythmically across the Paris canyon streets.

I Facetime endless footage of large groups of Wales fans singing the anthem and various other songs and post these to Facebook and watch the likes accumulate. I think of Richard unfriending someone for his endless posts about his child and think I might be regarded as something of a Facebook bore but in the ecstasy of our progression, do I really care?

We get drunk and get a taxi back to the hotel where I sleep soundly with mad dreams about Wales being in the quarter finals for a major international tournament, a crowd of people climbing up the Empire State Building wearing Donald Trump masks, King Kong appearing above it, wearing a comedy Donald Trump hairpiece. He's got into my subconscious this Trump fellah. I can't wait for this comedian to lose the election and disappear back to his Tower(6).

We leave our temporary home at dawn and drive back home stopping in the now familiar service stations where we fuel up on caffeine and granola bars throughout France and England.

We return home, convalesce, wash our clothes, do some work and watch several re-runs of the glorious games played so far during this dream month of June 2016, catch up on Coronation Street, Countdown and First dates, bore friends senseless about how amazing our adventure is – it's genuinely like nothing else matters – we're in some kind of suspended reality and we really don't want it to ever end.

I post the image of my crest taken by the German photographer alongside some stirring and emotional words that I composed in the aftermath of the Northern Ireland victory.

I've hit triple digits. Richard is suitably impressed yet more than a little envious, I can tell. I tell him his time will come; he just needs to compose something that pulls the heart strings of the nation or alternatively involves a dog invariably on a skateboard hurtling down some kind of perilous slope – check it out, Facebook is filled with them.

I vow to have a couple of days of detox and a few long runs; when I play my customary Monday night game of five a side I am blowing more than I have ever blown before. I nevertheless manage an impressive hat trick of nut megs (*) (two against the same player, a young man incidentally from France). Whilst emotionally I am euphoric, physically I am but a shell of a man.

I go to the Chester market and the butchers, Geoff and Dave are reluctant in their praise for our exploits and I watch the English flag hanging limply from the town hall, where famously the side of the clock that faces Wales doesn't have a face for, as I think I've mentioned before, the story goes, the English wouldn't give the time of day to the Welsh.

In the fishmongers we exchange fish puns and when he goes quiet I tell him not to clam up which is the best pun of the day and he should be batter than that with it being his trade I remark and tells him the trouble with the English is they have no soul and to be fair, he laughs as he chops the head of a smiling monk fish, telling me the cost of my fish is '20 squid.' Fair play fish man, you're eely not a bad sort.

Deep down, I don't think the majority of English fans want Wales to do well which is absolutely fine as I want them to do really badly. At least we all know where we stand. Let's not mess around here. We want to go further than you.

I pop into Baristas on Watergate Street for a flat white and exchange some banter with the proprietors Jacqui and Andrew De Looze who themselves have been out to France. Jacqui is proud Welsh and Andrew proud English. He says he's been supporting Wales and I think he's telling the truth but I'm not entirely sure. They live in between Hope and Caergwrle.

I notice a missed call from a number I don't recognise. I call it back and a woman with a French accent answers. It's the woman from the train station in Bordeaux. She tells me we must be very pleased and proud as to how the tournament has gone so far. I agree and say we're having the time of our lives.

She curtly passes on from the small talk as French people manage to do so well and she tells me the reason for the call is that she's taken in the cat and is thinking of making it a permanent home. The reason she is calling is she'd like me to name it. I picture it's tiny face through the bars in the carry cage. I picture it giving me the finger, telling me we're nothing more than a peninsula on the edge of England. The train in Bordeaux: it seems a lifetime ago.

"I'm honoured" I say.

She says it would be fitting with me finding it and taking the time to take it off the train. I say that's a lovely gesture and she says I don't need to make a decision right now but when I've given it some thought, I should call her back and tell her what I've decided. She hangs up and I picture the cat, meowing through the bars of the cage, the woman who left her, why she left her - was she too poor to look after her?

I catch up on Red Passion and read the thread on Danny Ward and the debate as to what we will spend the money on. One thing about being a community owned club, is a wonderful feeling that you do have a stake in your local club. Whether a supporters trust owned club can seriously compete in today's footballing environment of local businessmen investing serious money into the most innocuous of clubs is a real point of debate.

There's a discussion to be had as to whether we need outside investment or whether we can not only subsist, but actually succeed without somebody or a consortium pumping money in. A combination of the two is probably the answer but with the trust always needing to retain overall control to avoid those unscrupulous 'investors' with the wrong motives getting involved. Wrexham have been scarred more than most with the latter in recent years which has perhaps caused many to be sceptical of such investment. Anyhow that's a discussion for another time and if you ever want to dip into the debate, visit Red Passion and there'll always be a thread or two on the subject.

Going back to the cat in France and I should I suppose mention at this point, I have perhaps a slightly awkward relationship with our feline friends. A psychologist might quite obviously trace this back to the feline based deceit I suffered as a small child. There's probably a syndrome named after it but I've never told my therapist and never will.

Please Don't Take Me Home - A Cat Called Robson-Kanu

THE STORY OF FRISKY ONE

The story goes that I have a cat called Frisky which was unnumbered when I first had him. I was 5 years old. He was black and tiny and had a white smile under his chin. He was unremarkable in a cat exhibition kind of way but I really fucking loved that cat. He was in fact more like a dog than a cat. He would follow me to school and once through the gates, he's head off home, happy that I was safe. Then one day, he didn't come home. A week passed; then two. On a Sunday afternoon my parents returned from a trip out.

"They've found him, they've found him" shouted my mum and then my dad, cheering like Wrexham had won the European Cup.

They hugged me. It was like a massive Donald Trump Election Party. Even Nigel Farage would have been jumping for joy if he's been around then, delighted for the repatriation of our missing cat. They (my mum and dad, not Donald Trump or Nigel Farage) shouted, almost in perfect unison:

"We've found him, Frisky's alive" whilst hugging me, this unnaturally tiny cat, running through my legs, disappearing behind our hideous late seventies floral sofa and arm chair combination.

It was as close to being Frisky as Bobby Gould was to being Alex Ferguson or for those Wrexham supporters out there, Rob Oglelby to Sergio Aguero: you get the point - he looked absolutely nothing like Frisky. It was fraud on a massive scale. It was like voting to leave Europe based on massive

111

whopping black lies. A short sighted Cyclopes with an eye patch could see it wasn't my cat and the bigger issue, my therapist might argue is that this raised perhaps one of my earliest, even first of millions and zillions of dilemmas that soon become a life staple.

The dilemma that this created as a 5 year old was perhaps this: Do I pretend it's Frisky and embrace the moment, joining in their pyrrhic celebration singing "Frisky's back, yeah, go Frisky" or whatever filthy lie of a song they are now dancing to; or do I come clean; end this farce once and for all, grab The Imposter and shove him back in the car and take him back to wherever he's come from (not literally, as I couldn't at that age, you'll remember, drive myself) singing "fuck off imposter cat, go and pretend to be the pet of some other sad sucker."

I think back in this time (approximately 1977) this through for a moment, noticing beyond the TV show that was in the foreground playing out on mute: Last Of The Summers Wine, Songs Of Praise or something equally as mind numbingly depressing that always played out on a Sunday afternoon.

And remember, we only had three channels. Imagine that anyone born after 1985 - not only did we not have a mobile phone as a third limb, social media applications telling the world when to clean your fucking teeth but we could only watch TV on three channels between a specified number of hours, typically midnight signalling, with the playing out of God Save Our Queen that it was time to turn off the TV and go and do something less interesting instead: such as bed or sex or masturbation or a Jilly Cooper novel which covered some of the above.

And moreover, if you missed it, then tough shit, no plus 1 hours, no omnibuses, no catch up TV. No, that was it. You had to miss it and sit in school as they all talked how it played out. It really was like that. No you really have to go some to miss anything: it's actually impossible.

Anyhow, back to the cat anecdote: I looked at the cat cowering under the sofa, his cat eyes shining out on the reflection of the hideous lampshade. I made my decision. I couldn't be honest and hurt my parents feelings – they were after all doing what they thought was the right thing.

"Yeah, Frisky's back" I exclaimed, grabbing my parents around their collective mid riffs, as we all danced the most fraudulent of acts since Vinny Jones introduced himself as the national captain of Wales or again, for you Wrexham fans, Rob Ogelby introduced himself as a professional football.

So there it was, I had accepted the fraud, become an accomplice if you like and by the time Frisky Two as he became known many years later, became brave or perhaps hungry enough to emerge from beneath the sofa, I picked him up and accepted him as my own. This was first taste of being complicit to something that wasn't strictly right, the first of a series of White Lies that is something you sometimes as a human being just have to roll with. It's just the way of the world; get over it. By the way, what became of Frisky Two is a story for another time; we have football to talk about.

ICELAND

Iceland is a beautiful country: quirky, rugged, remote, extreme - like with many places, the landscape seems to infiltrate and reflect the people. They seem resilient, creative, can adapt to the conditions that surround and engulf them.

I've written already about the well documented rivalry between Wales and England so as we're progressing, watching England's progress, or ultimately, their lack of it, is, let's face it, after looking after themselves, the fate of England is often the next thing we look out for. My English friends think we have a massive chip on our shoulders and they're probably right, but it's something etched in your soul.

The next few hours are therefore, simply as beautiful as the Icelandic landscape itself, a Bjork ballad, a Sigur Ros instrumental, a geezer erupting into the pure blue sky, a waterfall making its way down a cliff face, a river whispering through a valley.

It's the big game: England V Iceland and I'm all ready for the action. I return home and settle down to watch what I am sure will be a one sided affair. I have a plate of fish and chips, a glass of Pinot Noir. I'm living the dream baby.

I apply plenty of salt and vinegar and then a liberal sprinkling of Lea & Perrins Worcester sauce (if you have never tried this on fish and chips, you need to get your head tested) wearing my Wales away kit and settle down to cheer on the Icelanders.

England take a predictable early lead and I finish my fish and chips and spend some time with the television in the background, checking my Twitter and Facebook accounts thinking that the next moment of any note will be a second England goal.

You can imagine my wonder when I momentarily jolted out of my social media apathy by the sound of astonishment from the English commentator, Iceland have only gone and equalised.

A series of Facebook posts pinball around cyberspace and it seems like the whole of Wales has erupted to see our near neighbours having what I am sure will be at that time, a temporary blip on their route to the quarter finals.

How wrong could I be.

A few minutes later the commentators astonishment appears to seep into borderline verbal assault against the English footballing establishment as Iceland take their deserved 2-1 lead.

The rest of the game is as tense as watching Wales play such is the desire for Iceland to prevail.

But prevail they do and social media is awash with not only anti-English sentiment but also the joys that victories from the underdog can only bring showing that sport does not always have to be as predictable as a Roy Hodgson press conference.

And talking about Roy Hodgson press conferences, the woeful array of pundits on ITV's a hastily convened conference is convened and Ian Wright's nonsensical drivel is interrupted by a solemn looking Roy reading what looked to be a pre ordained speech in the event from the filing cabinet under IF ENGLAND ARE KNOCKED OUT BY ICELAND OR WALES.

It is perhaps a personal failing but there's something hilarious watching the misery of English sporting disasters. They really should bottle it and sell it. It could perhaps be an antidote to the menopause or glandular fever or crabs. If you're feeling a bit off colour, watch England losing to Iceland; it really is comedy gold.

I watch the Facebook post of Steve Maclaren, one of the most lampooned England football managers ever (remember him haplessly parading the touch line in a dire game at Wembley during a violent rainstorm, sheltering under an umbrella), during the Iceland game as a pundit on Sky Sports, he's reassuring the English public that all is ok and under control and that England are comfortable and just as he's saying this, Iceland score, out of shot, and the camera focuses on his facial expression as he watches on a screen out of view. If you haven't watched it, google it, u tube it, do whatever you have to do; it will have you wetting you proverbial sides.

Next, the images of the Wales team celebrating the defeat are leaked on social media and many in England later use this as a reason to justify not supporting the last home nation left in the tournament. Alan Shearer to be fair is surprisingly magnanimous and says there's no reason why they shouldn't have celebrated this way. Hey ho. Whichever way you look at it, we're still in and you're not: playground stuff but I can't help it, it's how I feel.

We amidst this craving for temporary normality, discover that our opponents in the quarter finals (yes, say it again, the quarter finals) are the mighty Belgium, ranked as number 2 in the world. I try and gauge the opinion of those whose voice I respect and admire – the range on the spectrum goes from complete pessimism to those who believe that we could be Belgium's bogie team having not conceded to them during the European qualifiers having beaten them 1-0 at home and eking out an 0-0 away in Brussels.

I decide it's futile to speculate and rather concentrate on deciding which replica jersey I will be wearing for the big game and to find a suitable Airbnb for our upcoming two night trip which deep down I believe will probably be the last on this glorious journey. Not for the first time in this wonderful summer of 2016, I am not ashamed to say it but how wrong could I be.

THE JOURNEY TO THE QUARTER FINALS: FLIGHT TO PARIS AND AN ONWARD TRAIN TO LILLE

Tony collects me at 3.50am. I've spent the evening watching the re-run of the Slovakia and Russia games. I've deleted the Northern Ireland game for whilst it was of course an incredibly important victory, it was no better than watching Wrexham v Woking and the usual dross I am cursed with week in and week out.

Tony spends the first 30 minutes bemoaning the England national team and everyone connected to it. It is of course difficult for a Welshman not to rejoice in the woes of English sporting disasters and we are quite content for him to denounce his national team for as long as it makes him feel better about himself. The onslaught lasts for several junctions of the M56 and as we turn off for the airport, he wishes us well and declares that he sincerely hopes we get through into the semi-final and Tony being the great guy that he is, genuinely means it.

In the airport, we have our customary coffee at Costas with an energy boosting berry smoothie to provide the nutrients and vitamins that will sadly fail to pass my lips for the next couple of days.

As we go to board, the lady from the check in desk greets me by name and says "we've been seeing a lot of you over the last few weeks Andrew: I hope you'll be coming back next week."

Now that's service: Air France we salute you.

Please Don't Take Me Home - A Cat Called Robson-Kanu

I dream on the flight that I'm in a random changing room and I'm chatting to some decent enough celebrities of the time, probably the early 90s - Angus Deaton, before he got himself involved in shoving stuff up his nostrils, Nick Hancock before he became obsessed as did, seemingly everybody towards 1990s bloomer videos; you know, those excruciating cringe worthy video clips, typically filmed at the time, on hand held video recorders (before the advancement of video facilities on mobile phones - anyone under the age of 20 won't get what I'm on about) or on TV out takes that usually involved somebody swinging from a rope over a river when it would inexplicably break and the swinger would tumble hilariously head first into the river.

Then there would be the cat who just loved to jump into a recently decorated Christmas Tree, sending it toppling, hilariously over, usually into the toddler or small infant and better still, into a group of toddlers or small infants.

Then the dad, who having proudly both inflated (with his own lungs) and then filled (with his own hands) a swimming pool in a suburban garden (often in Australia) would decide to road test this new acquisition (bought usually at Walmart or some other massive home base shop, always on a Sunday morning under heavy strains of duress from the wife he doesn't much any more, like or feel any affinity with) stepping in by way of comedy stand up dive pose, sending, you might have guessed it, the water, tidal waving over the sides, flooding the adjacent lawn, flower beds, and better still, overflowing into a kitchen stroke open plan dining area that have long been the popular living area of choice, especially down under mate. I could go on and as there's loads of space to fill. I might as well.

From the TV out takes, there's always the one from Japanese Television where a mad cap game show presenter whacks over the head a contestant as a forfeit for losing a game where contestants have to wade through green slime in their swimming wear to reach a gold star that enables them not to have to spend a hour locked in a glass cage filled slowly with spiders, snakes and usually locust or cockroaches, depending on the season.

And then there the soap opera from Scandinavia where her boobs fall out of her dress.

And the newscaster who just can't stop laughing at the latest suicide bombing that's taken place in where was it; Baghdad or Basra or Bombay?

Yes, that's where he's at, possibly still adorning the comical screens of some low life satellite channel.

Anyhow back to the dream: there were others in the changing room, which going by the colour (lots of red), the crest and the familiar sound of the announcer, was the Oldest International Football Stadium in The Cosmos, the Racecourse Ground Wrexham including Mike Peters (my brother in law you will recall), his buddy, and by association my semi buddy (sometimes of course semi buddies become primary buddies and the previous primary buddy can sometimes, like an Indian Camel, literally get the hump, and fall away from being a buddy to you (neither primary not secondary) or to him or her) Billy Duffy (wearing the iconic image on his t shirt from the Pure Album which garnered hits such as She Sells Sanctuary and Edie), Kevin Radcliffe the previous captain of Wales' past generation and from a Wrexham perspective, then manager of the loathed Chester City football, not to be confused with the newly assembled Chester outfit known imaginatively as AFC Chester, Stan Boardman, the actually very funny (in person at least) scouse (you burnt down my Chippy) joke smith, Mickey Thomas (whose testimonial it might have been) and the scouse comic that eclipsed all other, the man with the tickling stick, Ken Dodd.

Well, in this dream scene, (remember most of the above did take place) I'm having some pre match banter with this assemble of celebrities all of whom at the time, would have fallen into the Categories of A-D and as is the case with the culture of CELEBRITY they will mostly (with the exception of Michael Peters and Billy Duffy) have shifted backwards in the CELEBRITY Pecking Order which typically is recordable by viewing the TV shows, event openings, the magazines that feature or don't as the case may be, the day to day vagrancies of their lives.

Some even, you may stumble across, have fallen completely out of the genre in its entirety and become, heaven forbid:

Taxi Drivers
Factory Workers
Waiters
Cheese makers

(This is not incidentally aimed at the former Blur guitarist who incidentally did or maybe still (ton) does ferment/harvest/ cook???? cheese in a Devon homestead on a form of sabbatical from contributing to the culture of rock and experimental music. He is still most definitely Category A *).

Tyre fitters
Jewellers
Shelf stackers

(I once came across someone who in fact went to a school local to mine who found Category B fame in a boy band which was ever so fleeting and perhaps the fleeting was too slow for them as the lack of talent demonstrated by this posse of posers was as woeful as this genre throw up (and I use the term literally)I won't name him, not for legal reasons as I suspect:

1- he wouldn't have the resource to pursue an action; and

2- I could, (should 1 above be misconstrued) fall upon the defence, albeit as shaky as a Richard Hope led defence, of 'truth' that, is as the Textbook 'Gatley on Libel' ably points out, a legitimate defence to an action of various types of defamation including slander (spoken word), libel (written word, the appropriate Tort in this instant) and the more obscure forms of injurious or malicious falsehoods).

Crane Drivers
Fishermen
Crab Pot makers
Swimming pool attendant
Bus driver

Cartographer
Stone dry wall maker
Mountain Guide (*9)

Anyhow. I digress: back to the dream.

I'm in the Racecourse Ground changing rooms is the recall, that's what the documentary or reality show to people call it, the gentle looping of the essential facts of the show that they repeat after every commercial break to remind our tiny pea brains as to what the very essence of the show is all about:

Debbie has been single for 24 years since the tragic death of her husband Barry from a freak agricultural accident

Debbie is now having completed her transgender operation now known as Darren and she's looking for love.

Yes I got that.

I can remember basic facts.

Anyhow, the brief "recall" is that.

I put on my kit. Michael Peters comes over, nonchalantly whispering something in my ear that I would perhaps have liked to have known earlier in proceedings.

He says something (for it has been blurred over the years) along the lines of:

"Just thought I'd mention it, but when the announcer comes

over, he'll say something like 'Hi Andrew, can you tell me what you're up to at the moment; filming another series of Cardiac Arrest or you doing a bit of theatre - I'd heard you were doing a play in Broadway blah blah de blah'- anyhow, when he does say this to you, don't whatever you do, under no circumstance pretend that you're not the Cardiac Arrest actor Andrew Lancel."

For the sake of brevity, I've pasted the relevant sections of Cardiac Arrest and Andrew Lancel below. If you skim read it, it will undoubtedly give you a better idea of this anecdote.

WIKI PEDIA

CARDIAC ARREST

Cardiac Arrest is a British medical drama series made by World Productions for BBC1 and first broadcast between 1994 and 1996. The series was controversial due to its cynical depiction of doctors, nurses, and the National Health Service, although it has often topped polls of the UK medical profession as the most realistic medical drama of all time.[1]

The series was created by Jed Mercurio (writing under the pseudonymJohn MacUre), a former junior doctor who had worked at a hospital in Wolverhampton, who drew on his own personal experiences to provide a more visceral, albeit wryly humorous, look at the NHS in the 1990s. At the time of airing, Mercurio was still working as a doctor.[2] Mercurio later went on to devise another controversial medical drama for the BBC in 2004, Bodies.

Please Don't Take Me Home - A Cat Called Robson-Kanu

ANDREW LANCEL

Andrew Lancel was born on 3 August 1970 in Rufford, Lancashire. He started his acting career in local theatre and as a cabaret singer. In 1993 he appeared in the film *Wide-Eyed and Legless* with Julie Walters and Jim Broadbent. He gained fame as the lead role in the ground breaking medical series *Cardiac Arrest* with Helen Baxendale. Since then he has become a well established theatre and television actor with a reputation for seeking controversial roles and projects. He was described as the most realistic doctor on TV and sporadically was TV's most hated man, after roles in *City Central*, *Bad Girls* and *Queer as Folk*.
He is best known for his role as DI Neil Manson in the long running ITV series The Bill, a role he played from 2003-2010, as well as the villainous Frank Foster in Coronation Street for which he won 'Villain of the Year' at the British Soap Awards.[2]
An accomplished singer for many years, Lancel has also performed his own one man show and has sung in venues including the Sands in Blackpool and the Royal Albert Hall in London.

In addition to acting, Lancel runs his own production company and has produced and directed numerous productions. In 2008 Lancel became a patron of the Unity Theatre, Liverpool.[3]

Lancel is also a regular panelist on the Channel 5 TV show The Wright Stuff and also covers the Pete Price Radio Show

Lancel is an avid supporter of Everton [4] and was an original ambassador of Everton In the Community, he is also involved in the Everton Collection.

In summer 2010 he played a prison officer in an award winning short film called *Inside Run*, directed by his former *The Bill* co-star Sam Callis which was shown at the BFI London Film Festival in October 2010.[5] Of the film, Lancel said "it's a long way from Manson and a joy to be directed by Sam."[5] He reunited with Callis for his next film, the award winning short film *Viking* co-starring Sophie Thompson.[6]

His numerous stage appearances include Adam Snow in the Bill Kenwright produced production of the world premiere of The Small Hand in 2014, Juror 3 in Twelve Angry Men in 2015, and his acclaimed performance as Brian Epstein in Epstein - The Man Who Made The Beatles.

It was announced in 2015 that Lancel would be portraying Brian Clough in a stage production of The Damned United.[7]

Now that you understand its significance it should make some sense.

So the bottom line; the crux, the heart of the matter is this:

I have been included in this celebrity based football match, part of the Mickey Thomas testimonial celebrations at The Racecourse Ground Wrexham, still at this stage of proceedings, a dream state, only on the pretence that I have to pretend convincingly to be an imposter, a replicant if you like. A complete phoney, a tosser, take your pick: an intruder who I have on several occasions during frequent bouts of insomnia that have plagued my adult life (I've tried Calms, Nytol, and am now trying some herbal horse tablets administered by an doctor from Bombay, the size of a small canoe (the tablet that is, not the doctor)).

I am pretending to be this, and you have to remember to appreciate the heavy weight of the task at hand, actor who at the time was Category A - make no mistakes of it. He was top dollar. He was starring in the most popular medical drama of its day, each episode watched by 5-6 million people, including in the Statistical Concept Of Probability, a large section of

A- this dressing room
B - the watching crowd of about strangely enough 5-6000
C - anyone watching any internet coverage, of which it transpired I have never seen any footage
D - my friends
E - my then girlfriend. (Go fuck yourself by the way)
F- my family

I am a massive fucking hoax.

It's embarrassing.

It's awful.

Now, I'm not beating my lovely and favourite brother in law up over this as this act, this offering, was completely and undoubtedly offered up in a spirit of complete unadulterated kindness. He knew how much I loved, no adored, my football club and so the opportunity to be part of the celebration of one of its stalwarts during his testimonial was something he had contrived, knowing that:

1-Andrew Lancel was due to partake in the game but due to unforeseen circumstances was unavoidably detained

2- I looked somewhat like him

3- I sounded a bit like him

4- I was similar in height and weight to him

5- I like him am a human being

6- specifically I am male of the human species as is he

So I am not berating Michael Peters at all: It remains a very kind gesture, on top, I should mention at this point, of several other very kind and in case I have not mentioned it, gestures over the years such as:

Taking me to Northampton when I was a student and thereby too lazy and poor to make my way to witness a rare bout of promotion to League One.

Allowing me to run on the pitch draped in a Welsh flag, dancing around aimlessly and moronically, digging up with my bare hands a piece of the sodden turf and putting it in my pocket with the intention of my planting it in the garden that I did not own, it thereby suffering the indignity of disintegrating into dust in that pocket of a coat I didn't wear ever again until several years later, stumbling upon it in a box of mixed miscellany, emptying the pockets and then sending it to Cancer Research or Help The Aged.

Taking me to Leyton Orient and watching us lose very disappointingly in a Play Off Final.

Not laughing as I cried as an almost fully grown man at above mentioned loss.

Buying me a guitar for Christmas when he first met my sister.

Not going crazy when after double digit hours still trying to teach me the three chords that made up Stand By Me by Ben E King that I never ever did master.

Taking me to watch Bob Dylan where I famously (to myself anyway) went to the toilet backstage, when who came out of the cubicle but a certain John McEnroe. As I entered the cubicle, he was at the wash basin, washing his hands. Due to the aroma as I entered I swear I said "John, you cannot be serious" before entering the cubicle. To be fair, he did laugh.

Allowing me to sing backing tracks on his first solo demo songs in a chateaux in France where I looked after a dog called Napoleon and a cat called Little Ginger.

Allowing me the opportunity of tour managing his first Exodus Tour of the United States, thereby also allowing me to miss a semester of land law.

Looking after my sister and helping produce two lovely nephews

Anyhow, back to the script and in particular you will recall, the dream, that I am having on an Air France flight to Paris.

I'm sat there now looking around the changing room in a moment that should fill me with joy and excitement. Instead I'm feeling like the phony who's just about to be revealed and shopped and shamed as the most terrible of frauds and as the announcer comes up to me and says pretty much verbatim what Michael has forewarned me, I say pretty much knee jerkily and perhaps it's my legal training.

So I respond pretty much seamlessly with the following retort to the Announcer, which forgive me for my arrogance is I think pretty decent given the circumstances:

"Well, as you might know, Cardiac Arrest was a pretty massive show and I think it's on record as being said by someone at the Beeb, that it really has, it's pretty accurate to say, surpassed expectations and not even looking for a pretty new genre, it really has hit the heights for a slot at that time, well we're all naturally delighted."

The Announcer nods his head like he knows all this, like he's a world expert on BBC produced hospital based dramas.

"And at the moment, whilst we all have, what I think I've gone on record as saying, a well earned break, as we did all really rack up the hours - (name removed for legal reasons) the producer was, I don't think she'll mind me saying, a real perfectionist, and if she wasn't happy with the take, then regardless of the hour, we would re shoot and if necessary re shoot again, infinitum."

The Announcer nods. He's trying to move on to Billy Duffy and news of the Cults big comeback tour that kicks off tomorrow in Rio.

But there one thing an Andrew Lancel imposter is.

He's unrelenting.

He's as Margaret Thatcher once commented, in that twattish way she seemed to have, so effortlessly mastered:

He's not for moving.

Not for Moving.

Absolutely.

"But during this, sabbatical of sorts (I say 'of sorts' making little bunny ear marks with my two fingers signalling quote marks which for some reason I feel are adequate and relevant) I am doing a little play, if any play on Broadway, can, I suppose be described as 'little' (those bunny ears again, oh when did I become such a premier league tosser) and it's getting well, quite a lot of interest already and we haven't even started rehearsals yet" I add, laughing now like a horse.

"Right, that's great" speeds the announcer, dragging his hand held mic onto Billy Duffy who might or not be dragging on a pipe, I cannot be sure.

(If this is nonsense Billy, I apologise, please do not sue).

Andrew Foley Jones

So next thing I'm running out the tunnel with the announcer mumbling on about Cardiac Arrest and a new series and a play in Los Angeles (I said Broadway you buffoon) and then he's on about The Cult and The Alarm and their new tour and album and something about Mike (and my sisters) new charity Love Hope Strength (it wasn't actually created then - that wasn't until later but I wanted an excuse to mention it and ask you to support it; it really does amazing work re cancer all over the world. Check it out lovehopestrength.org

The game passes in a whirl. I'm actually wearing a Wrexham kit. It's the thing of childhood dreams. I go out early and do keep me ups in front of the Kop. Despite the fact I'm a massive fraud, I want to suspend this moment for eternity. The game kicks off and Michael scores an own goal in the first minute which obviously creates ammunition for a lifetime of relentless piss taking over the years.

I settle into the play fairly quickly with a nice couple of simple passes.

My personal highlights are:

Nut megging Stan Boardman.

Fouling quite nastily Kevin Ratcliffe to the uncharitable cheers of the Racecourse faithful (remember he managed our arch rivals Chester FC).

Being told collectively by the Stoke City supporters housed in the away end that I was a wanker and that "I fell over...." as I was knocked to the ground by Kevin Ratcliffe in what on another day could be claimed to be an act of retribution and a definite penalty. My rather theatrical fall, perhaps driven on by the fact that I was of course pretending to be an actor; an act itself of unwitting irony in itself if you think about it, not helping my cause in the eyes of a very young, yet even then, rather twattish Mike Dean, whose preponderance in giving penalties of dubious qualities over those who some might say had an element of cast iron ness about it.

Hitting the bar with a 25 yard screamer which drew a momentary gasp from the 5-6000 people in attendance, followed again by a chorus of:

"Andrew Lancel... What a Wanker... Andrew Lancel ... What a Wanker...."

And so on.

Why I felt so aggrieved at such a verbal onslaught when I wasn't actually Lancel, still causes me some sleepless nights.

Perhaps psychologically, my impersonating of him was almost morphing my heart and soul into Andrew Lancel.

So when he had joy, I had joy.

When he had pain, I had pain.

When he was kicked in the shin by a rather naughty ex international, I was kicked in the shin by a rather naughty ex international.

When he was called a Wanker by an army of tattooed Potters (is that what they call people from the Potteries?) then I was too being called a Wanker.

With hindsight, If you have the opportunity to impersonate someone (and I don't mean in a brief Mike Yarwood kind of way), try it, it's pretty testing. I definitely think it's caused me some pretty long term damage.

I should add, that at the start of this chapter, I added, rather clumsily you might of noticed, a sort of disclaimer saying this was a dream.

I might of added this pretty late on in the process of penning this offering, my legal training making me wary, reticent even of possible legal principles that I may have offended by admitting to the acts of impersonation which although I can't actually specify with any academic certainty (despite consulting several hefty legal textbooks on subjects that I suspected may be of some relevance, to admittedly, the legal jungle that is the World Wide Web, which I urge you, as a lawyer, never ever, to rely upon).
It is awash with factual improbabilities, scammers, fraudsters, and as Alan Lewis a peer of the legal fraternity, recently only the other day, in fact, commented upon with a message of a picture of a mug which had the ample wording written across it in bold black lettering:

Google didn't train 6 years to be a lawyer.

So, go fuck yourself Google.

Please Don't Take Me Home - A Cat Called Robson-Kanu

So, whilst I don't think my inadvertent (and remember, it was indeed, inadvertent Michael Peters, please step forth of necessary) foray into the world of celebrity impersonation has actually breached any laws, I still would prefer to offer the defence if required that this was indeed, all one big, Bobby Ewing style dream and that JR wasn't actually shot dead and Crystal didn't in fact have shoulders higher than the Racecourse Floodlights and non of this really, ever did possibly happen.

The end point of this rather gratuitous chapter is I suppose, something that at the time may appear something of a disaster in the making can turn out to be a wonderful memory.

Anyhow, I wake from this dream (*8) and note with some surprise we have landed in France. It is time my friends to get ready for the biggest sporting event in our life times.

Andrew Foley Jones

THE QUARTER FINALS OF THE EUROPEAN CHAMPIONSHIPS 2016 – WALES V BELGIUM

We arrive in Lille via car. There's turmoil at the Tunnel and thankfully we sneak through and emerge the other side and find our way via google maps to our Airbnb and dump our meagre belongings and meet a man in a hotel bar for our tickets. We've used a reputable supplier but this man looks anything but and over the next 24 hours it's always on the back of my mind and I hope and pray they're legitimate.

We head off for some food and drink and in a quiet place off the square, we notice a Welsh couple sitting at a table in the corner. There aren't many football supporters in view so we join them and soon realise they're real characters. Llinos and Trefor, despite getting very drunk that night and losing all their belongings have since become good friends, part of the wonderful adventure that took place in June 2016.

Lille is just across the border from Belgium and it's effectively a home game for the world number 2 side. They're of course a great side, littered with international stars and they're more than firm favourites but one thing the trip so far has taught - expect the unexpected - and always lingering in the background, much for the Welsh as for the Belgians, is the fact that during the qualifiers they didn't manage a goal against us, with us achieving a courageous goalless draw away in Brussels followed by an unlikely 1-0 victory at home in Cardiff.

We meet Alan and Trefor and Llinos amongst many others and we head off on a pub crawl through the streets of Lille.

Please Don't Take Me Home - A Cat Called Robson-Kanu

Despite there being purportedly 40,000 Welsh in the French city, we're outrageously outnumbered and everywhere you look, there's a swarm of colourful Belgians, draped in ridiculous hats, gold, amber, brown and red swathed across the city. But as the day develops, pockets of Welsh red grow across the square, and it seems many have been stuck in the tunnel, choked with strikes and too many people trying to get through.

We do the obligatory swapping of hats and memorabilia and there's again, nothing but a carnival atmosphere, despite the comically high strength beer, the drunkenness is good natured and there's undoubtedly a firm belief on the part of the Belgians that they would, move comfortably past us to the Semi Finals. Oh you silly Belgians.

Getting to the stadium, we get lost in the confusion of the underground and our group is scattered across the tube network and we find ourselves with Mari, Alan's partner but Alan is elsewhere. We find a back street bar and try and track him down. The locals are perplexed by what our country actually is, not quite understanding that it wasn't part of England. We manage to explain the situation and they wish us well in our continuing adventure. I have a double espresso to take the edge off the Pelforth Brun and I am more excited than I have ever been for a game of football.

Alan emerges, very wet, as the heavens have now opened and we contemplate that this will only make the game even more interesting, with the thought of a Gareth Bale free-kick fizzing across the turf could be very interesting.

We leave the bar and find our ways to the stadium. Our dubious ticket arrangements turn out to be legitimate but we are sat amongst the hoards of Belgians. I won't again go too much into the detail of the game itself as you've all probably watched it over and over, it being etched in your sporting memory but you'll recall during the opening twenty minutes we were well under the cosh and trailing to a Belgian thunderbolt.

It looked like this could be the end of the adventure and we almost settle down to accept our fate. Then suddenly, that most important of scientific principles in sport - the momentum just starts to shift. We get a foothold in midfield, start to dictate the pace of the game and it really isn't a surprise when our warrior captain Ashley Williams smashes an equaliser with his massive hard head.

We mingle with some Belgians at half time and their pre match arrogance is visibly draining and as the second half gets underway we carry on controlling the game and when Robson-Kanu famously does his thing, with Sam Vokes steering an incredible header past the Belgian keeper, we are literally running down the steps of the stadium crying massive man tears of euphoria. Pockets of Welsh strangers embark in huge group hugs as we enjoy the last five minutes knowing we're going through to the semi finals.

We have some drinks in the square after the game and rather wonderfully the Belgian supporters provide us the travelling Welsh supporters with a Guard of Honour as we travel through the beautiful train station. Respect to you Belgians.

We return home and spend the day watching the reruns of the match before heading off to watch The Stereophonics playing at The Racecourse Ground, Wrexham.

It's then all about the planning for the Semi Final. Richard does his thing and plans out our route and I book our Airbnb. We then catch up on some sleep. Fair play to you Richard, your organisational skills are exceptional.

Andrew Foley Jones

INTERLUDE BETWEEN THE QUARTERS AND THE SEMI FINALS

We don't do very much in the time between Belgium and Portugal: we obviously wash all our forever appreciating memorabilia, read lots of social media, rack up some calories on Endomondo, give out plenty of love and attention to SFJ and watch endless re runs, on an infinite loop of the Robson-Kanu goal.

I become obsessed with trying to find some grey skinny jeans on E Bay and then in Gap in Chester. I end up buying some underpants which I gather can be back up for the trip to Lyon. I lose out on the George Berry replica strip but gather it was a fake in any event and think about the talking cat in Bordeaux.

It would at this juncture, make sense to fill you in on the story of Frisky Two, the rather tragic imposter who eventually became treated as my own despite my having to pretend he was something altogether different. He developed a personality of his own and during my teen years, we became firm friends and whilst he didn't follow me to school as Frisky One had done, he was a loyal, if not, a slightly more chilled out cat who I used to dress in a Wrexham kit and try and get him to return the ball by rolling it gently to him. He was rubbish but still we tried and it made me feel like what it would be like if you had an offspring who didn't like football - how would you cope with that?

Well, having got to that age where it was time for me to leave home, I had a tearful goodbye - to be honest he looked more interested in his plastic bowl filled with Kite Kat

Please Don't Take Me Home - A Cat Called Robson-Kanu

than my pending departure and as I waved him goodbye, sadly did I realise that would be the last time I saw my lovely imposter of a cat.

Cutting a long story short, on my return from University, I decided it would be nice of me to make my parents a toasted sandwich during their lunch break. They returned home as I was working the Breville Sandwich Maker, a signature dish of mine for which I was very proud.

As it was concocting a particular flavoursome cheese, ham and red onion combination, I literally chucked the cat out of the front door Fled Flintstone style due to him hindering my cooking by swerving like an eel around my legs.

The next thing, I hear a screech of a car braking suddenly and my dad disappearing around the side of the house, returning with a spade and a refuse bag and then disappearing with the same objects into the back garden.

As we five minutes later tucked into our wonderful sandwiches, he happened to mention he'd just ran over Frisky Two and had buried him in the garden. I was stunned, both my the cat death, but also by the fact that my dad referred to the deceased feline as Frisky Two - it turned out all along he knew that I knew it was a different cat and he and my mum would secretly also refer to it as Frisky One.

There's a lesson there if you want to try and find it. But fundamentally, the weird thing is, I've lost two cats to unusual circumstances over my life time so perhaps the discovery of the cat on the train – and indeed, not just an ordinary cat but a talking fucking xenophobic cat no less - it told me it was the reincarnation of Frisky One and Two and that Wrexham will one day be in the Premier League and Wales will one day win the World Cup. I didn't want to mention it before as it sounded, I accept, a little far fetched. But that's what it said as I walked from the train through the station. Despite its anti Welsh thing he had going on, his prophecy did, I admit, fill me with some optimism for the future.

Anyhow, back to the present day - I head over to my hometown of Prestatyn to see my parents: we drive down Gwaenysgor Hill which really does contrive one of the most amazing views you will see anywhere - the Vale of Clwyd spreading beneath us rising for the purple mountains of Snowdonia that dips like a sea monster into the Irish Sea, Anglesey lurking beyond the headland of the Great Orme. To the other side of the bay, the lights of Liverpool, the cathedrals clear in the distance – and on a really clear day, I remember as a child seeing the Isle of Man, the hills of Cumbria.

It's a place that always evokes a real sense of belonging, memories of heading up there with the anticipation going off invariably to a football match, returning afterwards either elated or full of doom and despair.

My dad adores Prestatyn; after humble beginnings there, having not had a great deal of luck, losing both his Irish immigrant parents as a child and then being adopted by a railworker from Prestatyn, he's made a life that he's grateful for and as you get older, perhaps it's the cycle of life, but I can see why he and my lovely mum loves it so much.
We have some dinner, watch the highlights of the Belgium

game and interestingly, I find some grey skinny jeans on E Bay and 'win them' – I'll be wearing them for the semi finals you'll be delighted to hear.

We talk about Frisky One and Two and the talking cat in Bordeaux and I agree to do some research into the Foley family tree. It would be nice to see how it all panned out and whilst my dad used to think it would be disrespectful to those who brought him up as their own, enough time has elapsed where he would like to know his and our very own history.

THE SEMI FINALS

Tony picks us up at 3:50 and is so enthusiastic about our adventure, I genuinely wish he was coming with us – he's been a huge part of our journey and is unwavering with his optimistic outlook on life which I love.

I naturally wear my new grey skinny jeans for the entirety of my stay in Lyon. We fly to Paris and on the plane there, I dream of the cat on the train and in the dream he tells me we will lose the Semi Final but we will rise again, reassuring me that Wales will win the World Cup, within my life time. He adds that Wrexham will also reach the Premiership and to keep the faith. I really need to talk to my therapist.

We arrive again at the airport and Richard tries his Passport Control Queue Evasion Tactic but it's as if they've been expecting him – we're immediately repelled to the back of the queue and whilst edging forward, we realise we're never going to get across Paris to the train station where we're supposed to connect for our onward journey to Lyon.

The train section of the journey is going to be problematic – we're at the wrong station and approaching the wrong train. As far as shambolic train journeys go, this is right up there.

We calculate that we really can't get across Paris in time so we have no option but to get on it. Somehow the man at the platform fails to notice we've got the wrong ticket and lets us through and we jump on the carriage and take some random seats in first class.

Please Don't Take Me Home - A Cat Called Robson-Kanu

We pass through the first couple of stops without any drama and decide to venture to the buffet cart for the obligatory café au lait and a couple of calming beers. It is here that we encounter the Most Dedicated Ticket Inspector In The Universe – Thierry.

He passes through the buffet cart and we think briefly about hiding in the toilets. He checks the tickets of some business types and then moves ominously onto us. Now, the worse case scenario here is that we are forcibly removed from the train at the next stop and even arrested – we've heard stories of this happening to several England fans -leaving us with a near impossible task of reaching Lyon and the Semi Finals.

Thierry takes the tickets, peers through the spectacles that rest menacingly on his unnaturally long French nose and looks up, before looking down again, longer this time, looking up, locking us with a stare only carried off by policemen, serial killers and French ticket inspectors.

"What is this?" he declares.

I look at Richard, he looks at me, I look at Richard again.

It's like a sketch from The Two Ronnies without any of the comedic genius.

We're just looking back and forth toward each other, me momentarily catching fleeting images that whizz by in the background. It's like we're watching a low level tennis match.

Someone needs to break the deadlock and it isn't going to be me.

Henry, looking down, fixing his stare on the ticket says again:

"What is this?"

You've just said that I might say or perhaps just think, noticing as he looks up, fixing his stare annoyingly on me, a bluebottle rattling against the window behind him, a swan on a lake, a man fishing - as I blink, behind my closed eyelids I picture home, SFJ, the xenophobic talking cat, wondering whether I'll ever father a child - Thierry breaking my melancholy with a tone of voice that has risen expertly, despite saying essentially a repeat of what he's declared already:

"What is this?"

Come on Thierry, you can do better than that.

I say exactly what I shouldn't. I say the one thing that is obviously going to get under the already irritated skin of Thierry The Most Efficient Ticket Inspector In The Universe.

I say: "It's a ticket Thierry."

He focusses all his Gallic authority onto me and I instantly feel like when you're getting a bollocking from a headmaster or a ticket from a policeman who just loves to make you feel like a useless little prick.

Please Don't Take Me Home - A Cat Called Robson-Kanu

Says Thierry; "I know it's a ticket – your huge problem my friend is – it isn't the correct ticket" smiling now, staring first at me and then at Richard. A seagull swoops on the morning breeze, hovering next to the window, as if observing this awkward human scene playing out in his alien world.

I need something from you now I try and communicate, telepathically to Richard - a part time judge who knows when to be stern. He looks back at me – Thierry has us both mentally in a state of flux.

I try and break through this psychological paralysis and think on my feet and decide sheer stupidity is the only way we're going to get through this.

I point to the crest on my Wales 'away' kit.

"We are so sorry Thierry, it's just we're not from round here – we've got to the semi final and in all the excitement we've managed to get ourselves lost and to the wrong station and to the wrong train – but you'll see we do have a ticket – it's just not for this train."

Richard adds his own dollop of daftness by adding:

"Yes, we've just got ourselves a bit confused what with all the excitement – if we need to pay anything extra just let us know, and we can sort it out that way?"

It sounds like he's trying to bribe Thierry (for legal reasons he was absolutely not trying to bribe Thierry).

Andrew Foley Jones

Thierry looks at me a little like a policeman did when trying to explain, whilst pissed, why I was trying to climb the Clock Tower in Rhyl at 3 in the morning. It just seemed the right thing to do officer is I think, how I tried to explain it, not altogether successfully.

Henry looks at me with – and the only way I can describe this – is like he thought I might have something psychologically wrong with me and that if he were to challenge it, he could have a mountain of social and administrative headaches to deal with. I could have mentioned the talking cat – that might have helped.

I add just for extra measure: "I'm just so confused with everything and like, if I don't get to Lyon and I miss this game, I don't know what I'd do."

Richard adds: "Me too" and we exchange the looks of two men who are trying to shamble their way out of a self imposed dilemma.

I think about creating some crocodile tears but resist and Thierry looks at my crest and says: "We like Pays De Galles – you play with a style and spirit – we love your Joe Allen and that Ledley with his dancing."

I start miming the Ledley dance. Richard joins in. Then a man in a pin stripe suits starts doing it and I joke you not - a Ledley dance routine is spreading right across the carriage.

Thierry might have jiggled his hips a little, although I might have made this bit up but he does then say:

Please Don't Take Me Home - A Cat Called Robson-Kanu

"We hope we play you in the final" he smiles, handing back our ticket, nodding to us as we walk away onto the next carriage.

The French Rail Authorities are notorious for their ticketing policy and we'd heard stories of people being arrested for not having the correct tickets so we've swerved a proverbial bullet there. Merci Thierry.

We reach Toulouse and not far from the airport our Airbnb - I'm sleeping in a bunk bed with Richard claiming the bottom bunk. I struggle up to the top and then realise it's quite a high bunk bed and I actually fear the descent that will need to made later on. Otherwise it's a beautiful apartment and a fitting place to stay on this, our biggest of occasions.

We meet Llinos and Trefor and then my good friend Wil Griffith and his son Hari and in turn his sister and her family and spend a wonderful afternoon with the hoards of Welsh and Portuguese in the winding streets of Lyon's city centre. I tell them about the cat and what he's been telling me but they clearly think I've lost it. Another George Berry replica shirt is on E Bay which I watch with interest. I'm tweeting and posting all sorts of stuff – I'm properly immersed in the occasion.

It's an incredible spectacle watching all this play out and scanning through social media, it seems the world is willing Wales onto victory. I really want time to be suspended: my only regret is that SFJ and my family can't be here.

I try and get hold of my childhood friends Phil Pamment and

Neal Lynch who've driven down for the game but they're running late and still haven't picked up their tickets.

By the time kick off approaches, we board the specially laid on trams to take us the half hour or so to the stadium perched in the suburbs of town. I think I am leading some beautifully melodic versions of the Welsh National Anthem but subsequent footage reveals I was not. It's amazing how alcohol can distort the senses.

At the entrance to stadium, the typically robust security check confirms we're not carrying anything that we shouldn't be and soon we are in our section, settling into our seats.

Inside we bump into our good buddy Andrew Rigby who's sat in the section beneath us. There's a feeling of disbelief as to what we're witnessing here as the players warm up. Unknown to me, Wil and Hari have managed to get pitch side and have a photograph taken with a certain Aaron Ramsey who of course is sadly suspended for this game after a second yellow against Belgium for an innocuous hand ball.

I won't go into too much detail about the game as it is of course well documented that the journey came to a rather unspectacular end, due it must be said, to the absence of Aaron Ramsey and Ben Davis and the mercurial talent of, like him or loathe him, a certain Christiano Ronaldo.

We salute our heroes in red after the game and then return back into the city centre and consider and reflect it was perhaps one game too many. We all gather, have a few drinks and say goodbyes to old friends and new and vow to keep in touch.

We head back to our Airbnb and go to sleep knowing, it was a game, on another day, we could have undoubtedly won.

I sleep and dream crazy things, George Berry having dinner with me and my family, the talking cat sat in his massive afro, a baby in a Wales kit sat in a highchair, Joe Ledley dancing with my wonderful mum.

We wake and collect our things and our thoughts and head for home.

THE JOURNEY HOME

We return home feeling like heroes. The nation feels galvanised. Everyone is talking about Wales. People are congratulating me. English friends in the main are pleased for us, for our experience, our achievement, our adventure.

We wake early, gather our meagre belongings and set off at dawn with the usual combination of every type of transport known to man: first a tube, then a tram and then a very comfortable train journey from Lyon Central Station, treating ourselves with a pair of first class seats.

As we travel through the beautiful French countryside past the scarecrows, cornfields, hay bales in every shape and shade, I close my eyes and recount the past few weeks, the people we've met, the patriotism that bounced through the airwaves in every city and town we have visited: of national song, the cheering, strangers from all nationalities sharing anecdotes, stories of their histories, their loved ones; the feeling that you are witnessing history in the making: all against the backcloth of national fervour that pulsed as a pumping heart back home as we travelled backwards and forwards inside some form of euphoric bubble.

Every game felt like it would be the last and this was the mentality carried every time we entered a stadium but despite this in the back of our minds the stories of Denmark and Greece and on a domestic level, Leicester City having just taken the Premier League title made you, very deep down in the improbable recesses of your heart and soul, made you question whether Wales could actually go all the way and lift the trophy.

Christiano Ronaldo ultimately put one of his mercurial studs into our bubble when he jumped like a stilettoed salmon and we ultimately didn't have enough to spring any form of turnaround.

The spirit of a team that was bigger than its individual components is something that without being melodramatic, simply stirs the soul. Wales have illuminated the tournament both on and off the field. We were expected to simply make up the numbers, have a party, be knocked out of the group stages. The team and its supporters have done something for the nation that will never ever be forgotten and have hopefully created a legacy for both football in Wales and perhaps from a cultural perspective, something far more wide reaching.

For many, Wales was simply a peninsula on the edge of England, a region scarred by dirty slagheaps and coalmines now defunct and disused with literature such as Richard Llewellyn's How Green Was My Valley and Alexander Cordell's Rape of the Fair Country Trilogy, famous exports such as Dylan Thomas, Tom Jones, Shirley Bassey, the Manic Street Preachers, Stereophonics and The Alarm.

Wales had now received publicity and a claim as a distinct nation similar to what traditionally, the Welsh Rugby Team have achieved but with football being a sport with a greater international audience, the publicity surrounding a major tournament such as the Euros is something no Welsh Tourist Board marketing campaign could ever have achieved.

Wales was trending on Twitter, was all over Facebook, the Visit Wales website was having millions of visits per day.

As well as galvanising a nation, the spirit and passion and togetherness of both the team, the management and perhaps most significantly, the supporters both in France and back home in Wales, gave the most positive marketing campaign that a country could ever receive.

This odyssey through France in June 2016 will be remembered for generations to come and shows that the underdog can still have its day despite a world in which sport is tumoured with greed and money and lacks the fundamental constituents that it should be founded upon – namely a group of individuals that work for each other on a level playing field that is the same for both competing teams.

Our journey around France has been simply euphoric, an absolute joyful experience. It is something that goes well beyond sport. A tournament that began so drenched in negativity: gut wrenching violence, political disarray back in the United Kingdom.

As I glimpse at the fleeting French countryside, the towns, the suburbs, factories, supermarkets, rivers, ox bow lakes, children waving from banks of canals, river boats with sails of every conceivable colour, on a sporting front, I conclude that Wales were one of the shining lights at Euro 2016. The players, the supporters and the Welsh media all collectively ensured that the slogan written along the side of the team bus declaring, "The Dragon Will Rise" did exactly that; the BBC trailers with Tom Jones and other famous Welsh icons capturing this snapshot of history so perfectly. On a wider cultural level, this small principality with a population of 3 million people has declared to the world that it is open for business.

I post some thoughts on Facebook and notice friends from my past together with those that I have met on this trip, liking and making comments. I'm not a great user of Facebook but it has been a wonderful medium for communication during this incredible summer.

On the way home, we book our flights to Vienna for the first World Cup qualifier in September and look at Google maps to see how long it would take us to drive to Moldova, Georgia, Serbia and ensure that our diary is free for the trip to Dublin to face our neighbours the Republic of Ireland.

I recall my highlights, in no particular order:

- The first game against Slovakia was something that will remain with me forever. The anthem, the sea of red across the stadium, Hal Robson-Kanu's winner.

- The children of the Wales players coming onto the pitch after the game and scoring into the empty net, their goals being cheered as much as the goals scored by the actual team.

- The Viking clap of the Iceland fans which will no doubt spread across terraces throughout Europe.

- Gareth Bale's free kick against England and the look on

their supporters faces.

- Going down an alleyway whilst lost in Toulouse after the Russia game and being confronted by a number of Russian fans who simply wanted to wish us luck in the tournament rather than to stick their KGB sponsored fists in our Welsh faces.

- England losing to Iceland in the last 16 game.

- The biggest highlight of them all, Hal Robson-Kanu's spin and turn and incredible finish to put Wales ahead against the Belgians. The euphoria of that moment will be difficult to beat.

- Joe Ledley's dancing exploits – probably the best dance routine you will ever see.

- Tony the Taxi driver for looking after us so gracefully and for sharing our adventure.

- My mate Richard for organising and sorting and for his great company.

- SFJ for putting up with me.

We arrive in Paris and despite some difficulty at Charles De Gaulle airport, where for some reason I have been booted off our flight, we finally manage to have me reinstated after I needed to prove that I did actually come out on the outward bound flight, having thankfully retained my boarding pass from that journey together with my match ticket stub and a train ticket from Lyon and as we board, the

Please Don't Take Me Home - A Cat Called Robson-Kanu

air steward who I have now met on several occasions makes me a coffee just the way I like it without me having to ask and tells me I should be proud of my nation's exploits, adding that he will miss the hundreds of Welsh supporters who have travelled through on his flights over the last month.

On the plane home, I recall some of the people I met. The Icelandic gentleman I met in Carcassonne; the man is familiar. I just can't place my finger on it and whilst he talks, I rack my increasingly intoxicated brain but reach no salient conclusion.

I indulge into another coffee and my mind won't let it go. I Google famous Icelandic actors. I scroll through what is admittedly not a huge roll call, but enough to go through say twenty faces. It's when I go, through them all again that I spotlight on the penultimate face; he looks way more polished, the background suggesting an awards event, perhaps a soulless hotel lobby in the centre of Reykjavik.

I click on and enhance the picture. I click through to links with his name on it; a film magazine, an Icelandic TV trailer. It's fucking him; the man we were drinking with in Carcassonne. He's only one of the most famous actors in the Nordic world. And whilst scrolling through the site IMBD I realise I watched him in a film subtitled about a man who is capsized out in a freezing Icelandic sea and somehow manages to swim to shore in temperatures that scientists say a human being couldn't in any way survive. That's where I recognise him from and you can't help but love the irony that he told me he was a fisherman.

As we land in a stereotypical rainy Manchester, the sound of Morrissey's "Every day is like Sunday" plays out on my iPhone and after going through the equally stereotypical queues in Manchester passport control, my passport will not go through the electronic automated gate and I then have to go via a human which is something I prefer anyway. Will there ever be a day where there will be no humans in supermarkets, petrol stations, passport control? I hope not. I prefer human interaction.

As we sit waiting for our taxi, I receive a telephone call from a French number. I answer it with some trepidation. The woman's voice on the other end of the phone is I quickly recognise, as the lady from the train station in Bordeaux.

"I just wanted to telephone you for two reasons: firstly really well done on reaching the semi-final – I was really rooting for you against Portugal but you should be proud of your achievement. Secondly, now I know this sounds pretty crazy, but with our pets, we like to give them some kind of christening ceremony. It's not a religious thing, more just a tradition. The point I suppose I'm getting to, is I really need to have a name for the cat as we're doing the christening ceremony this afternoon. Have you given it any thought?"

I smile and picture arriving at the train station in Bordeaux filled with excitement, anticipation together I suppose with just a dash of trepidation, stepping into the unknown and I remember looking at the cat in the cage left on the train and picking this up with his tiny face peering through the bars meowing, then talking and then purring as I handed it to the woman whom I'm now speaking to.

Please Don't Take Me Home - A Cat Called Robson-Kanu

 As I think back to that moment, a snap shot of different images from throughout the month of June 2016 flash through the projector head of my mind pausing somehow on the moment that Hal Robson-Kanu defied all logic Cruyff turning and spinning his way towards goal before smashing a left hook shot into the left hand corner of the net. I think of Robbie Savage's commentary, the running up and down of the steps of the stadium, the hugging complete random strangers, tears dripping down our collective Welsh faces. I say instinctively into my iPhone to the woman sitting in her farmhouse in Bordeaux:

"Robson-Kanu – I want you to call the cat Robson-Kanu."

A laugh emanates from down the telephone. She says: "I couldn't have thought of a better name myself – a great reminder of a wonderful moment – Robson-Kanu it is."

I smile and she thanks me for making the effort to hand in the cat and says that she will look after it and send me updates as to how he is getting on.

 "Au revoir" she says.

"Au revoir" I reply, terminating the call, tears dripping down my patriotic face.

Tony collects up from the usual spot in his typically punctual sense. He shakes our hands and then gives us both a big hug.

"Well done lads" he says "you should both be very proud to

be Welsh."

We sit in the taxi in silence and watch the English countryside roll by.

I check my phone, my Facebook status, my retweets, the Wrexham v Norwich football programme on eBay, the George Berry replica kit that I have been outbid on.

I return home, Welsh dragons hanging from the window to greet my return. SFJ gives me a massive hug and I fall into a sleep and dream of images of our French odyssey, drinking wine outside the Apollo, Gareth Bales free kicks against Slovakia and England, Joe Allen covering every blade of grass, Aaron Ramsey directing play, Ashley Williams leading like a warrior, Neil Taylor being an unlikely goal scoring hero, a wall of red singing and dancing throughout the towns and city centres throughout France. And finally, the last image before I wake is an image of Hal Robson-Kanu turning sublimely and smashing the ball into the net.

INDIA: SEPTEMBER 2016

I'm dropping biscuits into a lake and watching fish rise to the surface to nibble and fight and then disappear into the grey blue abyss. Some lily pads drift by, Keralan crows chatter and squabble over head, dive bombing discarded coconuts and jackfruit on the forest floor.

I watch the U Tube highlights of Wales win over Moldova as the call to prayer from the local mosque fills the dusk. There's nothing much more jaw dropping that this sound. It's the only thing after Land Of My Fathers that really scrapes at my soul.

The sun sets across the lake and sounds of a jungle coming alive as our day ends, another paradox of the relationship between humankind and animals. A chorus of cicadas rises from the trees and then suddenly ends, like a football chant.

I watch a documentary about New York City and a huge underground being contracted and sky scrapers reaching skywards. Mankind can be fucking marvellous when it isn't killing itself.

I check my Facebook, Twitter, e mail, E Bay, all these things we do automatically as a knee jerk, a human condition, as we evolve and surely one day will develop, a device - a tablet or more suitable, a mobile phone, an I phone 6s would fit nicely and there we will have it, we'll be a creature of three limbs. Imagine the fun we would have, the productivity, the destruction, the hand gestures one could give in time of traffic related rage.

Andrew Foley Jones

I'm trying to resist against this, the natural urge to check out the inane stuff that you are all doing. All I don't mean to be offensive with such comments, I mean, there's some great stuff on social media - seeing what your buddies are up to, checking the weather for that planned walk up Snowdon, how many rupees you'll get for the pound.

There's some really great stuff out there. And everyone can now be a publisher, a journalist - ideas can be percolated across the globe, both good and not so good. But there is some inane dross out there. I don't care that you're having your second espresso of the day. I'm not to bothered about Sammy being picked for the school team. And if I see another Dog On A Skateboard, fuck, I won't be responsible for my actions.

We visit a factory where they make ropes and carpets from the basic coconut. It's truly inspiring watching these people from the village who have created a co operative and make these items using rudimentary equipment. Truly inspiring. I naturally photograph it and Facebook it and watch the likes rolling in. As I say, it's part of our evolutionary tuning. It's how we're now wired. We all loved a retweet, a thumbs up from our friends, from strangers. We all love a bit of adoration in whatever form it may take.

I check in to the Twitter feed of Hal Robson – Kanu(*9). It says: I've got a club - I'm now at West Bromwich FC.

That's great news.

Stephen Halpin messages me to ask:

"How I'm going to cope with Aguero?"

"Haven't a clue what you're talking about?"

"Don't give me that."

"Seriously, I've not been reading the news."

Fantasy Football dilemmas.

Keep him for the two game ban or get rid.

I message Kinsella and he suggests he's not bothered this year but I suspect this may be a ruse?

Fantasy Football can seriously take over your life: be warned.

I watch something on Facebook about Dean Saunders telling an anecdote on Talk Sport about the day Brian Clough tried to sign him and he was hammered and did lots of weird idiosyncratic things. It's a funny story it really is: if you get the chance, it's well worth a read.

A journalist from the Guardian who also wrote a couple of books on Cloughie, does some investigative digging and after input from third parties who were actually in the room that day no less, then pipes in and declares the story to be complete bollocks and perhaps a ploy to enhance Saunders fledgling after dinner speaking career.

Bad form of its true.

Always liked Saunders as a player. Not the most naturally talented but always gave his all. Also liked him as a manager at Wrexham; had some charisma and generally seemed to want to do well for the club.

There is however always in the back of the mind the link he had with the regime that allegedly brought the club to within an inch of its life.
He's getting a predictable battering on Red Passion.

The up shot of what a lot of football fans don't perhaps appreciate is that for professionals employed in the sport, they don't typically have the association with a club that a supporter does.

There's always an exception but typically, it is their job, a way to pay the mortgage, provide for their families. If they have a good ethic and a pride in what they do, they should of course hurt when they lose or when they make a mistake or don't give their all. That's something all football supporters cannot forgive, not giving your all.

Where you ply you trade outside the sport, you can't help but think they the professionals are the privileged few, the lottery ticket winners of life being paid to play a sport that most of us pay a few quid a week to play ourselves, in five a side centres, sports centres, parks. A lack of skill, or technical ability can to an extent be excused; most players will, like a spirit meter, find their level. They should if nothing more, give the literal 110%. Anything less is inexcusable.

I've seen some pretty crap players over the years but the

ones who really get my goat are those who are crap but give no effort. They shouldn't be professional footballers.

I watch a man in the lake wading, chest deep, holding a crude rod made probably of bamboo. He looks up and acknowledges me as he concentrates on the ink back waters. I wave him farewell having watched him each morning going about his daily routine trying to catch some fish for his family. It's incredible the disparity that exists across our world. He won't be worrying about his retweets.

I go and see the Yogi to say goodbye: he wishes me well.

"You need to work on your Half Moon and of course, it goes without saying your Lotus is pretty shit, it has to be said: but overall, you've made some considerable progress."

I smile, stretching my arms above my head, pushing backwards, then moving forwards, trying to touch the palms of my hand against my feet.

"How about my downward dog and my cobra?"

He smiles.

"Pretty good huh?"

"And my half crab locust is something to behold right?"

"There isn't such a thing" laughs the Yogi.

"Well there should be" I retort.

Andrew Foley Jones

I'm going to miss this guy.

"And obviously, as I've told you before, you need to be patient - you won't be able to do everything overnight. Keep patient, keep doing the basics, practise them over and over."

I stretch back again and then forward, inching towards my feet. I couldn't get within 12 inches 2 weeks ago. As he says, gradual progress.

"People expect things too instantly. You need to respect the power of practise."

It's like a scene from Karate Kid. I'm really filling up here.

There are many lessons on life that are entwined within the foundations of Yoga. You can see that without reading the copious texts on the subject, or even Wikipedia. Maybe that's why he respects the exploits of the Wales national team over the past few years. Going back to basics, practise, over and over. Basics, over and over. Develop. Learn. Doing things the right way.

"Passion" he also urges.

"Passion is something you should show in everything you do: your work, your sport, your friendships, your relationships. Passion and pride in everything you do, is a fundamental."

He points to a statistic on his I phone. Look at this, he says:

"Moldova were 5 places above Wales in the FIFA World

Rankings just 5 years ago. Now you're 154 places above them. Progress. Incredible progress."

I nod.

"And better still, look at this."

He points to a Facebook post by a man called Alan Lewis who it only turns out is my mate Alan Lewis who the Yogi is following.

Alan has posted a table showing Wales above England in the world rankings.

"Doesn't it look wonderful" says the Yogi, beaming as brightly as the morning sun rise.

"It's great doing well, but come on, isn't it lovely to be better than the English."

We laugh and he starts, no joke, doing the Ledley dance, singing 'As long as we beat the English' by the Stereophonics.

He says that domestically Wrexham will come good again and I understand the comparison I say.

"They will have their day. You're building the right way; right from the very setting of solid foundations. It takes time. You have to be patient."

Not with Gary Mills in charge I say rather than think.

"Bryn Flynn as Director of football and that lad Darlington as manager" suggests the Yogi and I couldn't call it better myself. If he doesn't want it, you could do worse than Dean Keates I add.

"Look at your Swansea, your Hull, your Bournemouth. Yes, you might need an element of outward investment but that can only come from a solid foundation which in my view is fan ownership. I know there are some who think it is the wrong path but save for someone coming in with an open cheque book, it is the only option. And do you really want to be a plaything of a sugar daddy? You've seen the dangers of that."

Indeed we have.

We both smile and then break into huge laughter as we point towards the post on his page.

"Anyway, I thought you couldn't stand social media" I say.

"There's good in everything" he says, opening up a page that says:

YOGA CLASSES DIRECT FROM THE BEACHES OF INDIA

With him on the Yoga stage, a sun rising beyond his head, his eyes clasped closed as he hovers, incredibly in a Lotus position.

"I can now run classes to all over the world" he beams "and they don't even have to come to India."

"You massive sell out" I respond giving him the international sign language for he who plays with himself.

He gives it me back but adapting it so the gesture is gesticulated back and forth from his forehead area and even this seems more appropriate done from someone with a decent posture and stroking motion that is, very much in love with a decent breathing stroke.

In.

Out.

Knob head.

In.

Out.

Knob head.

Now breathe.

And.

Relax.

I must remember this and administer it whilst playing Chester or 5 a side, after I've nut megged Michael Farrissey for like, the umpteenth time.

"Let's hope Gary Mills is open to learn. You know what, I am guessing he isn't and I am thinking that you will be way off promotion this season. I think he'll be sacked by Christmas. The Board have got themselves into a bit of a pickle but they'll soon see that he's effectively idle. He wants to stay at home and go on the sun bed and have pints. He doesn't really give a shit. I'm a pretty good reader of people - I'm a bit psychic - get it from my mum. I see things. Once he's gone, you'll need to get someone with young ideas, the science, the nutrition - all that stuff we've talked about before. The return of Jordan White will be like a new signing. I think he will get you lots and lots of goals. But beyond all that, you must get rid of that Mills character."

I truly hope so. I'm starting to completely doubt the ethos of our manager. I think he's a fraud. I'm hearing stories and whilst not one to jump onto rumours, there's definitely something seriously wrong: the lack of training, the lack of scouting, the lack of discipline, the inability to play people in their best position. It's unreal.

"And, on the international stage, I think Chris Coleman just needs to ensure he has a Plan B and even a Plan C and even a Plan D as there will be times when you are without many of your, let us say, without being disrespectful to the other players, your key performers."

I nod in agreement.

"I mean, I'm not saying you were lucky in France, but until the Semis you did manage to keep the same team more or less, with of course, Hal and Sam alternating often depending on

Please Don't Take Me Home - A Cat Called Robson-Kanu

the make up of the oppositions defence and general formation. I know Jonny Williams also alternated a little with other midfielders but more or less, you had your best squad to choose from."

You're so right I don't have to say.

He continues, his clear blue eyes focussing now on the shifting tide, drifting towards the shore under the power of the earth's gravity.

"And let's be honest, you deserved a pot of luck as you've had some rotten misfortune in the past. Joe Jordan in 1978 and the Welsh FA, greedy fuckers as they were back then chasing the dollar and deciding to play it at Anfield - what were they thinking - then there was the handball down at Ninian again against the Jocks and then of course, Paul Bodin missing the penalty - and why in the name of Ganesh did Rushie not take it - then there was the play off defeat at home to Russia. I'm not generally one for retribution, but boy, it was nice to give them a good beating at the Euros - back to Moscow boys, off you go."

He laughs as a fishing boat comes close into shore, a man in a Chelsea replica kit with Drogba on the back, hauling in a net with a catch of shimmering whitebait, their scales glistening on the rays of the morning sun.

It's funny but when these fishermen are far out in the ocean you can spot the greens and blues and reds and whites of their garments and you romantically picture these as shawls of locally crafted materials created by their wives and mothers as they toil in the inky black sea at night. Only to realise when you see these fishermen arriving at the nearby port at dawn that the colours are invariably replica jerseys of all the major European football sides.

As they dollop King fish, anchovies, mahi mahi, tuna they size of a thigh of Wayne Rooney I saw, Manchester United, Chelsea, Arsenal, Real Madrid, Barcelona, Paris SG, Liverpool, even Motherwell, the gut stains of sliced up calamari like they'd been head butted by Duncan Ferguson down a dark and desperate Glasgow alley.

Would you believe it?

The Yogi tells me to keep in touch.

"I'll give you a free years subscription if you agree to like my page and retweet and like everything I post" he smiles.

As I've said before, no matter what you're outlook on life, we all like to be the subject of a little adoration. We all would like to have a terrace crammed with adoring face, swaying this way and that, like the fronds of a thousand palm trees dancing to the soothing samba of chirping King fishers, white tails, sea eagles - as we turn toward the centre circle arrowing our fingers downwards, behinds our back, pointing in the direction of the name emblazoned across the top of our jersey.

I nearly even did it myself you'll recall, albeit under the guise of a name that wasn't even mine despite the wobbling crossbar. Somethings perhaps just aren't meant to be.

Please Don't Take Me Home - A Cat Called Robson-Kanu

I give the Yogi a hug.

He tells me to keep practising and to remain patient.

"I'll be watching your progress, domestically and internationally" he says.
"You watch Joe Allen flourish now he's getting regular first team football. He should play further forward you know, in the No 10 slot."

Yogi absolutely adores Joe Allen.

Well, don't we all.

We fly home via the benign yet remarkable country of Dubai. The remarkable engineering involved in creating a city out of a city is simply stunning but there really is something excruciatingly sterile about the place which means I can never take to it.

It's the absolute oxymoron and I want to get out of the heat and the wealth and another Bentley and a Lamborghini whizz past on the empty highways. It's a surreal place.

I listen to the Wrexham V Sutton game via the links on the Red Passion web site. It sounds dire. I imagine the friends I attend with, sitting through another horrendous display. It angers me, frustrates me. This Gary Mills needs to fuck off now.

I write a column for the Daily Post. It's my turn this week. I write it very quickly, right on the final whistle which I notice with amazement is greeted with boos and jeers. I wonder if Gary Mills will be brave enough to do his victory parade around the pitch, fist pumping as he does.

I don't typically agree with booing. It's just something I don't feel inclined to do. I know the constraints I'm dealing with. It was like when Wales played under Bobby Gould. If anything would make me boo that would have been it. However, I can sympathise. Even though I'm unavoidably not at the game, this distance almost crystallises my thoughts.

It's a stark realisation that we really do deserve something better than this. I can accept at the fifth level of football, there's going to be something of a talent gap but not being able to do the basics, trapping a ball, passing it to the intended target and more than anything, looking like you couldn't give a crap.

That's unforgivable.

It's funny but I've known some footballers and I wouldn't be as disrespectful as to put a name to the comments, but get this, they didn't actually like football: they just happened to be good at it. but they both always appreciated the need to give their all, to show passion and respect to the supporter.

At the moment, there appears to be a terribly corrosive combination of lack of talent and lack of appetite and respect for the club.

What I write is set out in the footnotes (*10). There's also a letter to the Board that I write on the day that unknown to me, he is sacked. My letter never got published and again I've included it in the footnotes to this book (*11).

PROLOGUE: NOVEMBER 2016

The great news from a Wrexham perspective is they've got rid of that awful fraud Gary Mills. I've just returned home from a 3-1 win against the richest village team in the world, Forest Green Rovers. They're everything that's wrong about modern football – a wealthy benefactor that's distorting the economic landscape of the league with disproportionate wage structures, creaming the best players from the lower leagues whilst playing in front of dismal attendances – they brought 64 supporters as a team top of the league. Whilst the amount of people watching you shouldn't be an automatic barometer of success, there's something that feels wrong that a team with no history, no soul can just pop up as a plaything of the wealthy and suddenly go on a folly up the football leagues which will last as long as the money or the inclination of the benefactor.

The team are still short on quality but there's an intensity to the play that simply wasn't there with Mills. Since Dean Keates has taken over there's a desire, a hunger to play for the club, to close down, to do the ugly part of the game. With the addition of some quality over the coming months and the moving out of certain players who simply aren't of sufficient quality for this level, we'll stabilise this year and kick on next. Longer player contracts for those who show promise is a must if we are to have any plan to succeed. Such a plan also needs to be put in the public domain to a certain extent: the supporters, who of course are the custodians of the club, need to have information, feel they belong to something which has a plan for the future.

People with knowledge of the football business need to be involved and a full time, properly paid professional with experience in the sport needs to be involved in some capacity, fronting a board of supporters who share the necessary skillset to help run a football club.

There needs to be a clear financial plan with some innovative ways of making money: using the stadium for the asset that it is – day to day activities such as conferences and then concerts in the close season coupled with some kind of initiatives where supporters can acquire different levels of packages in return for different pricing structures. Some might say this is elitist but if a sector of the demographic who follow the club can afford to pay more for a different offering, then why not encompass this.

Wales' World Cup qualification is stuttering somewhat but with a group that is wide open, a couple of victories and we'll be ok. It's been a bizarre year in so many ways with on the sporting front, Leicester winning the Premiership and Wales reaching the Semi Finals of the Euros and the top ten of the FIFA World Rankings. Then in politics you've got Brexit and then Donald Trump. It certainly is the Era of the Underdog.

Anyhow, it's time to bring things to a conclusion – my publisher Don Hale is shouting at me for the final proof. I hope you've enjoyed this snapshot of the past few months: as I said at the start, it really has been a simple story of two friends who journeyed to watch their team, simply expecting some fun, the once in a generation opportunity to watch their nation at a sporting event but who incredibly ended up watching their team reach the semi finals.

As Don has put on the back of the book, this is indeed a story that extends beyond football: a commentary on modern society, the irrational joy of beating England, an absurd obsession with social media, hilarious anecdotes - a talking cat found on a train, an imposter at a Mickey Thomas Testimonial (remember this did actually happen), a chance encounter with a Russian Supermodel, eating turkey sandwiches with an international rock star, an Indian Yogi obsessed with Joe Allen - all against the backdrop of often comical attempts to navigate Wacky Races style around France.

Wales defied sporting logic when during the Euros, staged in France in 2016, they inexplicably reached the semi finals. A nation erupted - patriotism reached new bounds: a branding exercise no tourist board could ever account for, a feel good factor that spread like a dragons wing across a principality, so often in the shadows of its English neighbour, unexpectedly grabbing the international spotlight.

""*Football is in the blood, in our soul. It is part of our lives, it can determine, often subliminally our mood, our productivity. It's a major part of our DNA, it's part of what makes us what we are.*"

As I sign off, we've had the wonderful news that a new life is on the way: we've just returned from a three month scan which confirms a baby is due in June 2016.

The conversation in the Countess of Chester Hospital went something like this:

Me: can I have the baby born in Wales?

Midwife: you can have the baby born wherever you like but as you live in Chester, it would be our recommendation that you have the baby born here.

Me: OK no offence but I'll probably drive over to Wrexham or Bodelwyddan.

Midwife: no offence taken – I am in fact Welsh so I understand to an extent but really, someone can be born here and still be brought up Welsh: it really all depends on what you teach your child.

Me: ok, let me think about it.

So if you see a black car speeding down the A55 or the A483 through North Wales, sometime during early June 2017, please let me through.

There's also the issue of a slight calendar clash with a trip to Serbia for a crucial World Cup Qualifier booked in just two days after the due date but we'll talk about that again.

CYMRU AM BYTH

ENDS.

INDEX

CALENDAR JUNE / JULY 2016

Key dates	Activity
Thursday 9th June	Packing and planning for trip
Friday 10th June onward train	Flight from Manchester to Paris – to Bordeaux with night in Air BNB
Saturday 11th June	Stay in Bordeaux and go to match V's Slovakia
Sunday 12th June	Day in Bordeaux
Monday 13th June	Flight from Bordeaux to Paris and onward flight to Liverpool (Air France strike / Air BNB in Paris booked but not used for 3 days)
Tuesday 14th June	UK
Wednesday 15th June	UK
Thursday 16th June	Flight from Manchester to Belgium with onward trains to Lens for the England game
Friday 17th June	Overnight return coach / ferry / coach back to the UK

Please Don't Take Me Home - A Cat Called Robson-Kanu

Saturday 18th June	UK
Sunday 19th June	Flight from Manchester to Paris with onward flight to Toulouse and train to Carcassonne and stay in Air BNB
Monday 20th June	Train from Carcassonne to Toulouse and final group stage game against Russia
Tuesday 21st June	Flight from Toulouse and Paris and onwards to Manchester
Wednesday 22nd June	UK
Thursday 23rd June	UK (BREXIT)
Friday 24th June overnight stay in hotel	Drive to Folkestone with
Saturday 25th June and watch the last Northern Ireland	Drive from Folkestone to Paris 16 game against
Sunday 26th June	Drive back from Paris to UK
Monday 27th June	UK
Tuesday 28th June	UK
Wednesday 29th June	UK

Andrew Foley Jones

Thursday 30th June	Drive to Folkestone with tunnel and drive onwards to Lille to stay in Air BNB
Friday 2st July	Day in Lille including a lunch with Alan Lewis and friends followed by the quarter final game by Belgium and stay at Air BNB in Lille
Saturday 2nd July	Drive from Lille to the UK and go straight to watch Stereophonics at Racecourse Ground in Wrexham
Sunday 3rd July	Very hungover in UK
Monday 4th July	UK
Tuesday 5th July	Flight to Paris with onward train to Lyon and stay in Air BNB
Wednesday 6th July	Day in Lyon followed by game against Portugal in semi-final
Thursday 7th July	Train from Lyon to Paris and flight home following the slight catastrophe at Paris airport where I was bumped off the flight
Friday 8th July	Back in UK

Footnotes

*1: Connie Beauchamp:

Constance "Connie" Beauchamp is a fictional character from the BBC medical dramas Holby City and Casualty, portrayed by actress Amanda Mealing. She first appeared in the series six, episode 35, "In at the Deep End", broadcast on 1 June 2004,[1] and appeared in Holby City's sister show Casualty multiple times, having already appeared in crossover Casualty@Holby City[2] episodes. Mealing continued her role as Connie until the thirteenth series of Holby City,[3] departing in the 28 December 2010 episode "Snow Queens".[4] Connie's role in Holby City was that of Clinical Lead of Cardiothoracic Surgery in Darwin, and Joint Director of Surgery.[5]

It was announced on 23 July 2013 that Mealing would be reprising her role as Connie, but in Casualty.[6] Connie Beauchamp was introduced as a consultant in emergency medicine, in March 2014, over three years since her last appearance in Holby City. Later, in June 2014, Connie's role within Casualty became Clinical Lead.[7]

*2: For all those ornithologists out there, please note that I have shamelessly made up the names of many of the birds that circled around the India and I therefore take no responsibility for any incorrect descriptions or indeed birds that I may have inadvertently made up.

*3: Believe me, I am very much in the school of thought that men wearing replica football kits are not socially acceptable. However, after my experience in France in the summer, I do now accept there are exceptions.

*4: These are all characters from Red Passion. As I say elsewhere in the book, contributors to a fans football forum such as Red Passion should be congratulated even if you don't always agree with their views – they are the lifeblood of a football club.

*5 Pelforth Brune: is a English Brown Ale style beer brewed by Brasserie Heineken in Marseille, France

*6 Molasses means is a viscous by-product of refining sugarcane or sugar beets into sugar. Molasses varies by amount of sugar, method of extraction, and age of plant. Molasses is primarily used for sweetening and flavouring foods. It is a defining component of fine commercial brown sugar.[2]
Sweet sorghum syrup may be colloquially called "sorghum molasses" in the southern United States.[3][4][5][6] Similar products include treacle, honey, maple syrup, corn syrup, and invert syrup. Most of these alternative syrups have milder flavors.

*7 Sigur Ros: is an Icelandic post-rock band from Reykjavík, who have been active since 1994. Known for their ethereal sound, frontman Jónsi's falsetto vocals, and the use of bowed guitar,[8] the band's music is also noticeable for its incorporation of classical and minimalist aesthetic elements. The band is named after Jónsi's sister Sigurrós Elín

*8 eeeeeeekkkkkk he only went and bloody won it.

*9 Mountain Guide in Snowdonia and a short and highly unsuccessful spell in Northern Africa where rumour has it (reliable source yet still won't name in light of aforementioned potential libel action) he led a small group of Japanese business men into an area renowned for its political instability with rival tribes frequently skirmishing with each other over local land ownership and feuds typically fuelled by the stealing of a prized goat or a chieftains sexy daughter and theft of one or both of the above.

This would really get the juices boiling and this Guide walked them right into the middle of it, leading to a banker (be very careful at this juncture, not to mistype or mis-say a consonant from much further on in the alphabet) from Kyoto to spend 4 long and difficult months locked up in a cowshed in a village deep in the Atlas Mountains, fed only with a diet of goat droppings, mashed juniper berries, raw harken fish (found in very deep remote fresh water lakes fed by melting glaciers that shift through the region as slowly and painfully as a John Terry marshalled English defence) and blood cakes made from scorpion/sheep piss/eyes of harken fish.

The Banker was eventually freed after the Japanese Government offered the local tribal chieftain a 5 year supply of Yak Yak Bars, a then very popular confectionary bar consisting of nougat, peanuts, white chocolate and those hundreds and thousands that you used to have scattered over your ice cream and jelly when you were a kid at a eighties birthday party.

The Chieftain soon grew tired, it is reported of the bar as one of its apparent side effects was extreme forgetfulness, blurred vision, impotency and very severe halitosis.

The Japanese Banker purportedly after 12 months back in his Kyoto life: his bland apartment, his bland flat chested wife, his poor quality wifi, his minor Category B-E celebrity status, a developing dependency of Starbucks Latte with an extra shot and a drip of cinnamon, a hooker called Dimitri who it seems, properly infiltrated his self conscience, convincing him to actors public displays of indecency, including:

Revealing his testicles (not his penis) to shoppers riding the escalator in one of his city's endless shopping malls.

Posting postcards to neighbours in his apartment block inviting them all to A Testicle Party with, you might have guessed it, a pavement shot of his testicles emblazoned across the postcards front elevation.

Going to a Yoga class and whilst in a semi moon position, trying to lick his own testicles.

Painting his testicles with badly replicated Murals of famous scenes:

The Ceiling Of The Sistine Chapel
The Crucifixion of Christ
The Loch Ness Monster
The Starbucks Emblem

Please Don't Take Me Home - A Cat Called Robson-Kanu

Well, the result of this weird stuff was by all accounts as diagnosed by a team of the regions top dog psychotherapists as a very rare form of Stockholm Syndrome where broadly speaking a captive begins to love the capturer.

*10 This wasn't in fact a dream but a true event that did take place back in around 1995. I called it a dream for legal reasons as I'm not sure if there is law on impersonating someone at a celebrity football match. In case there is, it is a dream.

*11 HAL ROBSON-KANU
You all know the song. We sang it all over France, all over Wales. Let's be honest, he's always been something of a championship level player. Hard working, good at sticking his muscular arse into the crouch of retracting defenders, fearful no doubt of their manhood. He certainly can hold a ball up. His Wikipedia profile says:
Thomas Henry Alex "Hal" Robson-Kanu (born 21 May 1989) is a professional footballer who plays as a striker for West Bromwich Albion and the Wales national football team. Although he primarily played on the wing, he has more recently been used as a Forward. Notably to great success for his national team, Wales in the UEFA Euro 2016 Championships, where they made the semi-finals, and he has made clear that this is now his preferred position. He is expected to play in this position for his new club side West Bromwich Albion [5]

Robson-Kanu started his career as a schoolboy at Arsenal but was released at 15 and joined Reading. After graduating from the Academy in 2007 he spent time on loan at

Southend United and Swindon Town before returning to Reading and making his first team debut in 2009. Limited to mainly substitute appearances during his first season, he became an important member of the squad appearing regularly during the 2011–12 Championship winning campaign. He made his Premier League debut in 2012 and went on to score 30 goals in 228 games for the club before his release in 2016.

At international level Robson-Kanu initially represented the country of his birth, England, at under-19 and under-20 level. In 2010 he switched allegiance to Wales, the country of his grandmother, playing for the under-21 side before his debut for the senior team against Croatia on 23 May that year. He scored his first senior international goal against Scotland in March 2013 and his second against Cyprus in October 2014. Robson-Kanu was selected to represent Wales at UEFA Euro 2016, where they made the semi-finals.

When you see him interviewed and no disrespect to your stereotypical footballer, but he's not like a stereotypical footballer. He's eloquent, handsome, he looks like he could be a actor in a BBC period drama. He has a sardonic humour. He could do with having a slightly Welsher accent, but hey, that's just nit picking.

It's well documented that he was the only player in the entire tournament to not have a domestic club. An amazing statistic and one which must have brought some insecurity as he flew out for a month in France.

His cult status was clear in the early stages of drinking in Bordeaux during the opening game. The slow, lyrically resistive chant of his name over and over doesn't sound like the receipt for an instant hit, but these are terrace anthems we're talking about, not complex viola chord arrangements. As lyrics and melodies go, it's not going to trouble the Mercury Music judges but hey, they favour rappers playing Iranian xylophones, goat playing tambourines so you never know.

It goes like this:
HAL (pause) HAL (pause)
HAL ROBSON KANU
HAL (pause) HAL (pause)
HAL ROBSON KANU
Repeat to fade

The winning goal in the opening game was never going to win goal of the season but it was absolutely crucial to the ultimate success of the campaign. It took off the pressure. Three points was the bedrock of our progress.

His second goal of the campaign was of course goal of the tournament. Literally. It has been well documented elsewhere. I'm sure you've all watched it over and over. He's now got a club. West Bromwich Albion. Playing at the top level can only be of benefit to Wales. Good luck to the legend that is Hal Robson – Kanu a man with a cat named after him.

*12 Subject: DAILY POST: A LETTER TO MR MILLS
Dear Mr Mills,

Let me introduce myself. I am a humble supporter of

Andrew Foley Jones

Wrexham Club. I've been going since 1979. I've been a season ticket for the majority of those years.

The start of the 2016 season, Wrexham FC's eighth in the fifth tier of English football has been, on the playing side at least, one of the most controversial and perhaps, amongst supporters at least, one of the most divisive of all.

There are as in most debates, different schools of thought which have conceived, two classes that a supporter may broadly fall within.

Using terminology from the most popular fans forum Red Passion, these categories may simply be divided as follows:

The Happy Clapper = the person who always sees the glass half full. A Happy Clapper will only ever boo at Halloween or at scary movies. A Happy Clapper will clap even in the most dire of circumstances including last minute postponements, inept defeats, the inability of players to do the most routine of footballing activities.

The Frother = the person who always sees the half empty and literally "froths" at the earliest signs of a problem. A Frother will boo more than clap. A Frother will boo even in victory. A true Frother will every day, fear Nuclear Armageddon, a land attack from North Korea, or worse still, relegation into an abyss of even deeper oblivion.

The divide is causing practical problems. Supporters are arguing at games and banter on the fans forum is becoming more and more venomous. It's a bit like BREXIT.

Please Don't Take Me Home - A Cat Called Robson-Kanu

I like to think of myself as a realist; perhaps somewhere in the middle ground. I try and remain optimistic. I remember the confines that we are dealing with: limited budget, fifth tier of football etc. I know I'm not going to be served up Michelin starred football every week. Such is life.

However, I nevertheless do expect something a little bit better than cold beans on toast (and not even Heinz). I've got to say, without sounding in any way "frothy" that it is becoming increasingly difficult to find anything to be optimistic about our recent performances. You might say that we're not in a bad position. Mid table with a game in hand. I think we all know we have been extremely lucky to have the points on the board that we have. It feels like we have found our saturation point and that things may indeed only be worsening.
Our Football Club is in the blood, in our soul. It is part of our lives, it can determine, often subliminally your mood, your productivity. It's a major part of our DNA, it's part of what makes us what we are.

The club has been saved by the supporters; some memories from the history of the club make grown men cry. We all have our own favourites. Porto away, Arsenal of course, there are so many. I've often contemplated whether supporting a more successful club would have any impact on how I turned out as a person. We will never know.

I've tried to not care. I've tried to give it up. But like Bakewell tarts (Kiplings, no imposters), Marks and Spencer's Crinkle Cut Crisps, sweet and sour king prawn, gin - I can't give it up. And sometimes when I come home, declaring "I am never going again" kicking at the proverbial cat, my better half smiles and knows it will pass.

It's an addiction of sorts.

We all have opinions; we all think we could pick the, right players, right team, right formation, know the precise time to make the game changing substitutions.

We're entitled to such thoughts, it's part of the joy, the frustrations, the inherent culture of being a football supporter.

But we all know deep down, it must be more difficult than we think. It's not a computer generated game.

Being a footballer, is, speaking perhaps on behalf of most football supporters, something of a privileged position, something that is born from natural talent and then hard work to maximise that talent.

You have achieved much in the game, particularly as a player. You played at the very top. You played under one of the most iconic managers of all times. You must have learn an awful lot.

You arrived at the club as something of a marquee signing.

Your first season began with us playing some, and I don't wish to appear, melodramatic here, the most aesthetically and effective football I have seen for many decades. It was at times, unbelievably good. It was a pleasure to watch. It really was.

Then. The wheels somehow came off spectacularly.

Something seemed to go drastically wrong, especially around Christmas. Rumours, as they do with a passionate and caring fan base, circulated, speculating about training methods, a drinking culture.

It is of course difficult to know what is true and what is not. But clearly something went wrong and it affected terminally our chances of success.

The season limped to a languid end.

Pre season as ever was fuelled with optimism. Wales' incredible exploits in France, helping people in the Principality (yes, even those in the north) believe that perhaps, just perhaps, this could be the year.

The signings were unspectacular but the majority were willing to wait and judge by performance.

A pre season with odd opposite followed with a strange set of opening results and in particular, very strange performances, some incredibly poor, almost unwatchable.

Winning and being booed off was something I have never seen before and I'm pretty sure something that must of been a real weird experience for you.

I wonder if from where you sat, it looked as bad as from the stands.

I know you might be constrained by factors that we the fans, know nothing about.

You might have a terribly feeble budget.

You may be unable to afford the players you want to sign.

You may be left to shop in the bargain basement.

If so, I feel for you. It must be terribly difficult to deal with such adverse constraints.

I am a humble supporter. I have no coaching badges. I played football at University level and like to think that I have a reasonable knowledge of the game. I'm not an expert. I accept that.

If I were however the football manager of our great club, these are the things that I humbly think we need to think about:

1- play a player in his natural position; I don't understand the trend of playing someone outside his preferred position. In exceptional cases, yes, you can find someone is better suited but I don't think we have the luxury of tinkering in this way.

2- play a 4/4/2 formation; I think at our level, simplicity would be the best policy.

3- sign certain players on a 2 year contract; I know there's an argument that you don't want to be saddled but surely this would concentrate the mind when recruiting. It is soul destroying when a decent player leaves after a year. Indeed, this policy makes it seem farcical to talk about anything beyond a 1 year plan.

4- target a certain number of players to progress from within the club to 'grow' alongside other more experienced players. Supporters feel an affinity to home grown talent and obviously the odd exceptional talent can be unearthed which can bring in exceptional longer term income.

5- extend contracts as soon a talented player is identified (Curtis Tilt and Hamza Bencherif for example)

6- study the opposition if we don't already

7-maximise training methods and perhaps publicise (without giving away any trade secrets) what actually goes on in training as supporters are dubious that we are training competitively, compared to our rivals.

8- indulge in question and answer session with supporters

9- off load some deadwood

10- sign 2 central midfielders

11- then play a settled side and let them get used to each other

You may say it's non of my business, indeed none of anyone's business and that you rightly have autonomy over all things relating to the playing side of the club.

However, such is the nature of the business that I think the supporters, the very life blood of the club should to an extent be listened to in some forum.

I genuinely hope you manage to bring success to the football club. I've never met you but you seem to be a decent human being with a passion for what you do.

You don't owe anyone anything, you are after all just doing a job. It just happens that your job determines the mood, indeed, the life, of a collective group of very passionate people.

In your industry you must have very thick skin. Indeed being a top player under a tough manager you must have heard it all. We are a relatively small fish but we care as much as any larger club.

It must be tough. But ultimately it's also really tough at the moment being a supporter.

Please Mr Mills, please make us a successful side.

Please make us proud again to be a supporter of our great club.

Everybody, after all, wants the same thing.

Yours Sincerely,

*13 DAILY POST: A LETTER TO THE BOARD

Dear Board

It's been difficult writing columns this season. I used to write a lot about formations, who should play where, general football support stuff that is debated by every supporter in every club right across the globe.

It's now become impossible to write about stuff like this as the football has become so pointless, no inanely terrible, I simply don't possess the vocabulary to fill a page. It's absurd. In 44 years on this wonderful planet, I've never experienced such a standard of abject woefulness. Anyone who knows even a ???? about football can see this is terribly worrying. It's Sunday League.

I was chatting to my nephew about stuff, life, love, football and he asked me why Wrexham were so rubbish.
I said it wasn't an easy question to answer.

He said someone had mentioned Wrexham were not so lag ago in the same division as Swansea and Hull and why were we now five divisions below.

Ask me one about UFOS, Loch Ness, the Yeti, why humans continue to be so unfathomably cruel to each other - give me a chance here.

Well I explain we've had a bit of bad luck with bad men who didn't look after the club like they should have done and we've made a few bad decisions and things just haven't worked out like we should and he seemed to accept this and then he hit me, right between the eyes with a thunderbolt that couldn't have been hurled at me any harder than if it were by the devil himself.

The question was:

When someone isn't doing a good job they lose their job and are replaced by someone who might do a better job.

Why is Gary Mills still the manager when Wrexham are doing so badly.

He's 9 and I can answer most stuff he throws at me; but here, I'm momentarily mute.
He wore a Wrexham shirt I bought him to school and people laughed at him.

They're questions I just cannot answer. It's sublime. The manager was hot property when we appointed him and so, presumably ad the upper hand in negotiations. But really, so much so that he has us by the balls. Because that's the only rational reason why he is still at the helm of this hapless ship.

I completely agree that fans should not necessarily know everything; however, a fans owned club with the pedigree and traditional that we have in the situation that we now find ourselves in, should be presented with some information, some guidance and comfort that the custodians of our great club have some plan to get us out of this disaster.

Now before I go on, I know you're doing this voluntarily and this makes any form of criticism appear incredibly dishonourable, disrespectful almost. You deserve a huge amount of credit and recognition and should in no way be individually targeted for abuse.

However, conversely, the veil of respect for what you do in your own time cannot allow apparent chinks in the armour to be ignored. It would be surreal, negligent, call it what you like, to allow the current predicament to go without as much of a wittering.

And as they may say, it's not the criticism that will kill us, but the apathy.

As I, a simple man who views life as pragmatically and objectively as I can, the all encompassing problem we have at the moment is that most rational (not a crazy minority that so often plagues football clubs that will undoubtedly do possess) is there is a complete disconnect between the club and the supporter.

I know decent people who have followed the club for years who simply feel they are being disregarded, disrespected, treated like fools.

There simply has to be some effort to heel the fracture that is spreading before our bloodshot eyes; in a cartoon, the ground would be zigzagging, a road runner would drop dramatically into one of the crevasses left behind.

Without some action, there's a real and present danger that the support will tumble to numbers never seen before which could eventually exterminate the club.

Sub plot to this disconnect include:

Mills is simply not endearing himself to the supporters - he needs to seriously think his script for interviews as what he is coming out with is simply adding petrol to the embers.

Everything points to a training regime of a part time club; days off after victories, the feeling that the manager's desire for time at home, is shaping how often we train, prepare.

There is no affinity between the players and the supporters; the lack of local players and a manager who lives a long way away really doesn't help.

Constantly playing unbelievably negative football.

Playing players out of their natural position.

I'm not a big advocate of changing managers every five minutes and I was fully behind the appointment at the time but it's clearly not working. When something is fractured, it has to be mended; otherwise, terminal arthritis will forever plague.

Without appearing melodramatic, we appear to be at what they call a "trigger point" - a moment where history can change pretty dramatically: the edge of an ice age, a meteor the size of Gary Mills sun bed, a political revolution, the demise of an empire. It all sounds a bit frothed up but really, I think we're in the edge of the proverbial abyss.

It honestly feels like we're part of a social experiment; a new reality show where we as Wrexham FC supporters are being tested to the bounds of loyalty and simply human respect.

Believe me, there's a point where despite the fact that it's in our blood, it's in our soul, the vast majority will simply say enough is enough and channel our energy, emotion, our hard earned finances into alternative pursuits.

I used to love going to the games, it was one of the highlights of my week. Now, I am starting to feel apathetic, unbothered; it's a strange emotion.

You are selling a product; the product is defective.

The customers need to see an attempt to getting it fixed; and quick.

Yes, it's fine to rant and froth and boo and hiss - it's what humans do when they're properly peeved. But the question we all need to consider is put simply what do we know:

There are perhaps the following options-

(a) Continue as it is.

(b) Install a new management team

(c) Install a new management team and change the constitution of the board.

Whatever needs to be done contractually, I think it now needs to be done.

I would go and try and recruit Darlington or someone like Dean Keates to work with an experienced head like Brian Flynn.

We need a management that indulges in modern practises, coaching methods, science, and who portrays an ethos of professionalism right through the fabric and culture of the entire club, from the shop, to the kit man, to the ticket sellers right through to the management and players.

Gary Mills gives the impression that he managed to attain success without all this modern stuff and probably with a pint and a fag after the game but the world is now completely different.

He's probably at nice guy but he s a nice guy who doesn't give the impression that he give a monkeys about our club; we can't afford to waste any more time.

We need a shake up; a professional paid up chief executive with a history in football who can lead others in making the stadium profitable and can steer the club forward with the footballing side left in the hands of someone like Flynn and Darlington.

Please Don't Take Me Home - A Cat Called Robson-Kanu

Please do the right thing: please get rid of Gary Mills – he simply doesn't care about this great club. Please then appoint someone who does.

Yours Sincerely,

Andrew Foley Jones.

Andrew Foley Jones

THE END

Please Don't Take Me Home - A Cat Called Robson-Kanu

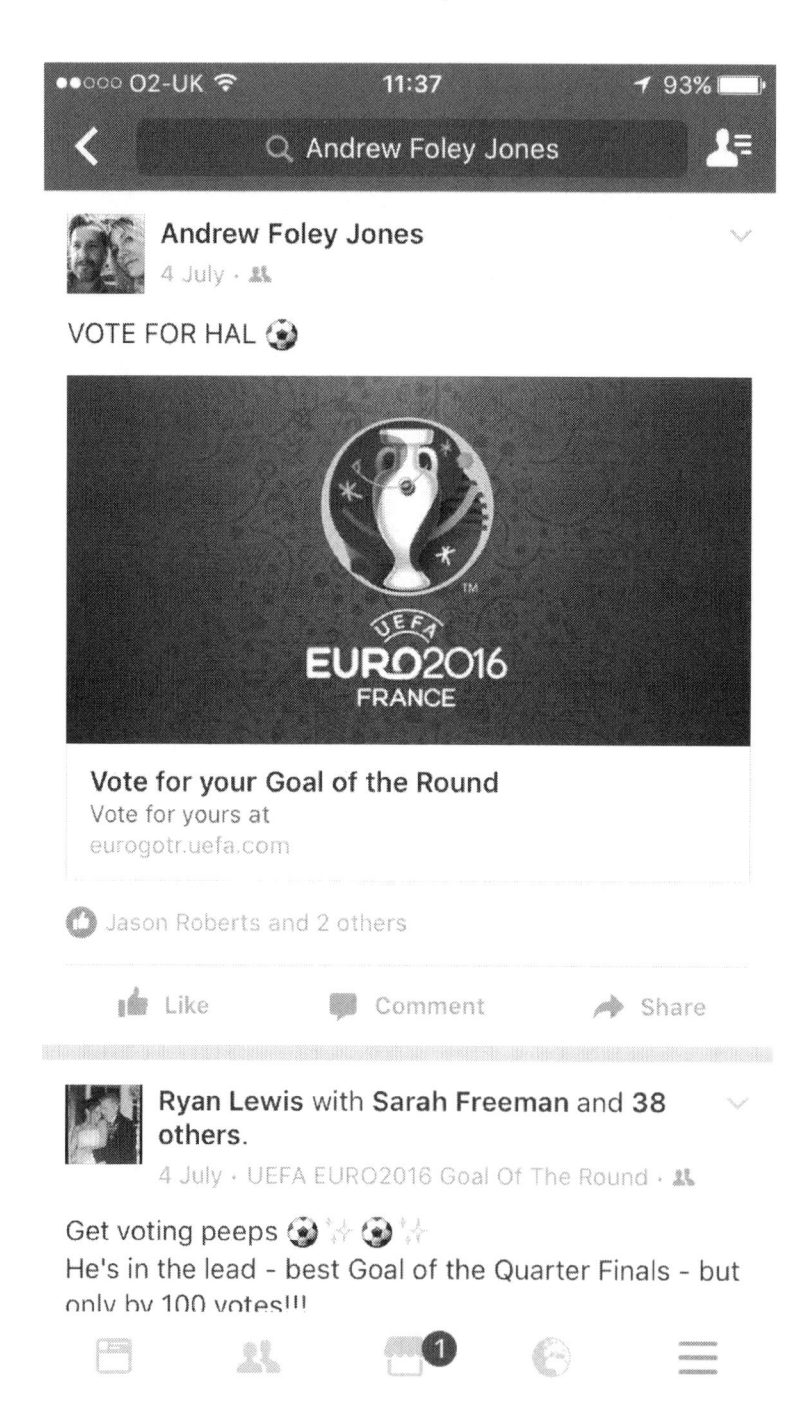

Andrew Foley Jones

●●○○○ O2-UK 🛜　　11:37　　✈ 93% 🔋

< 　🔍 Andrew Foley Jones　　👤≡

Andrew Foley Jones
4 July · 👥

VOTE FOR HAL ⚽

Vote for your Goal of the Round
Vote for yours at
eurogotr.uefa.com

👍 Jason Roberts and 2 others

👍 Like　　💬 Comment　　➡ Share

Ryan Lewis with **Sarah Freeman** and **38 others**.
4 July · UEFA EURO2016 Goal Of The Round · 👥

Get voting peeps ⚽✨⚽✨
He's in the lead - best Goal of the Quarter Finals - but only by 100 votes!!!

206

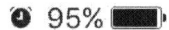

Please Don't Take Me Home - A Cat Called Robson-Kanu

•••••○ vodafone UK 4G **22:46**   95%

‹   **Tweet**   🔍

⇄ Colm O'Gorman Retweeted

Ryanair ✓
@Ryanair

To celebrate another #Brexit, for one day only, bring a 3rd bag on board (must match this one) #ENGISL #RyanairEuros

Reply to Ryanair, Colm O'Gorman

Home   Notifications   Moments   Messages   Me

Andrew Foley Jones

Please Don't Take Me Home - A Cat Called Robson-Kanu

Flood warnings have been issued in England as the whole of Wales pisses themselves laughing.

WelshnotBritish.com

Andrew Foley Jones

Please Don't Take Me Home - A Cat Called Robson-Kanu

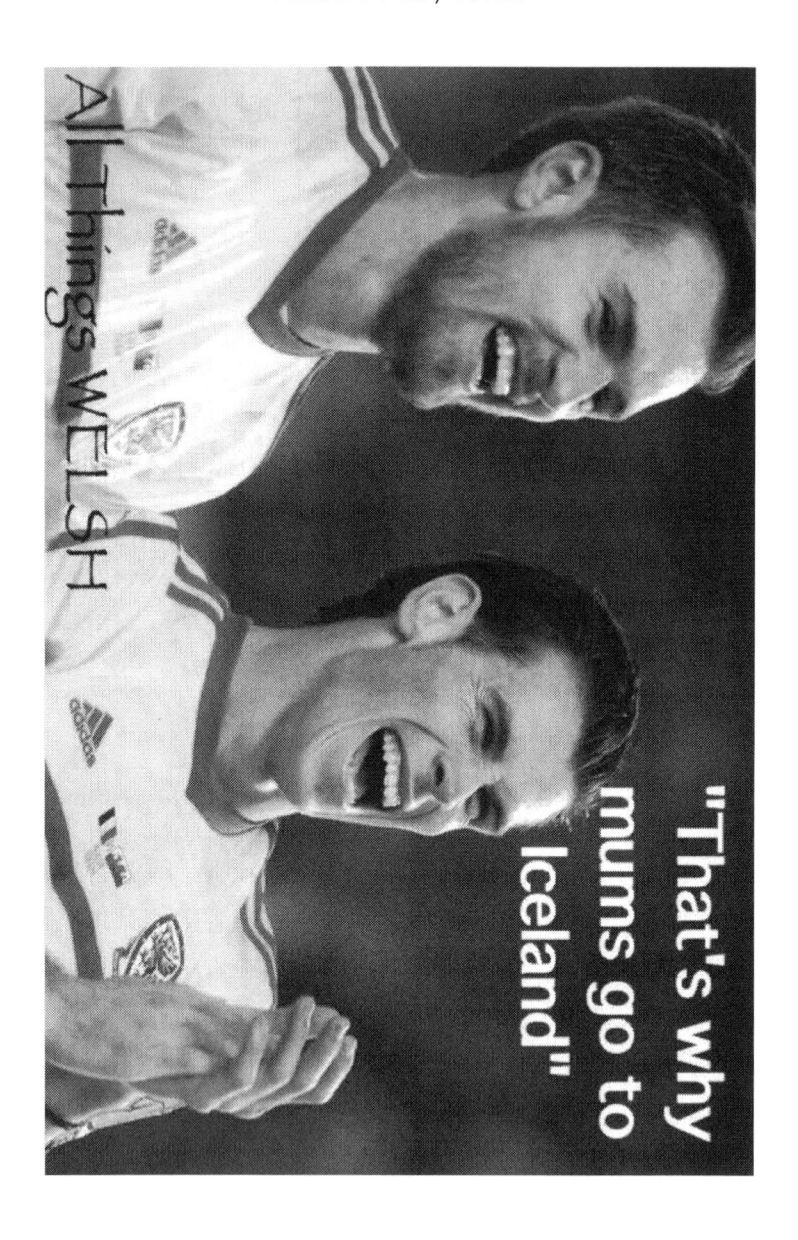

Andrew Foley Jones

Please Don't Take Me Home - A Cat Called Robson-Kanu

Andrew Foley Jones

Andrew Foley Jones added 2 new photos.
21 June · Halton

Just to confirm, it was her hat I was wearing. Can't believe the camera man zoomed in on her and not me.

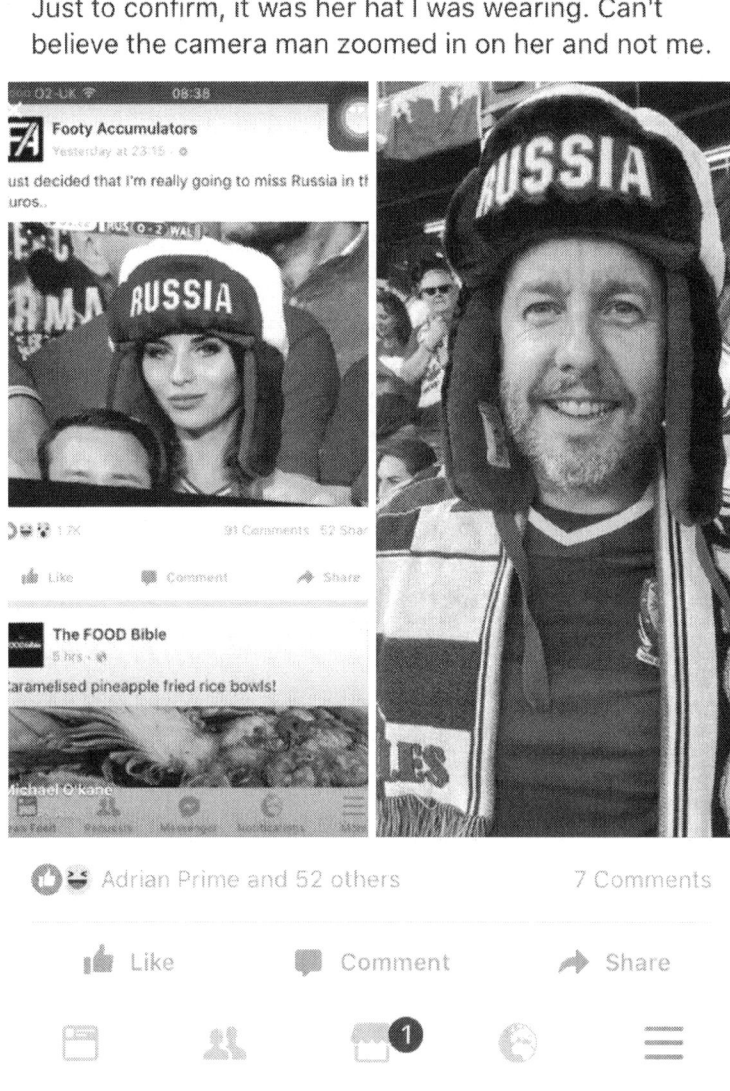

Please Don't Take Me Home - A Cat Called Robson-Kanu

Andrew Foley Jones

Please Don't Take Me Home - A Cat Called Robson-Kanu

•• ○○○ O2-UK 🛜   11:43   ✈ 93% ▮

Andrew Foley Jones

Jules Jones Peters added 9 new photos — with **Peter Jones** and **6 others**.
20 June

THERE ARE NO FRONTIERS
That we can't cross tonight
There are no borderlines
To keep us apart... 🖤⚽

176   19 Comments 5 Shares

Like   Comment   Share

Andrew Foley Jones

Please Don't Take Me Home - A Cat Called Robson-Kanu

Andrew Foley Jones

Please Don't Take Me Home - A Cat Called Robson-Kanu

Andrew Foley Jones

Please Don't Take Me Home - A Cat Called Robson-Kanu

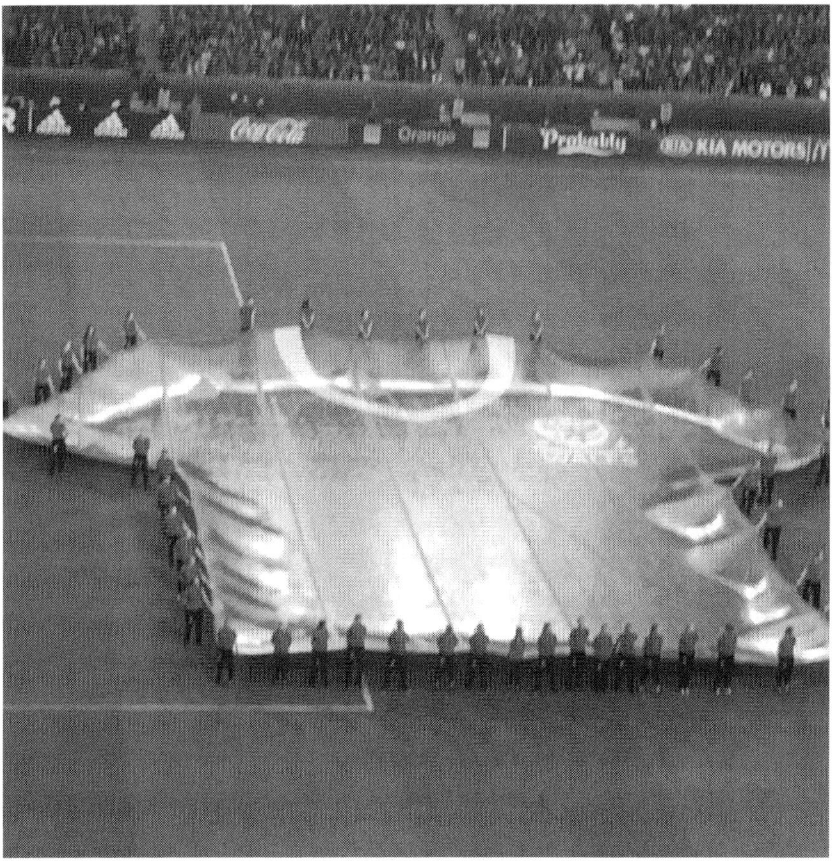
Coca-Cola
KIA MOTORS

Please Don't Take Me Home - A Cat Called Robson-Kanu

Andrew Foley Jones

Please Don't Take Me Home - A Cat Called Robson-Kanu

A reporter once asked Zidane:

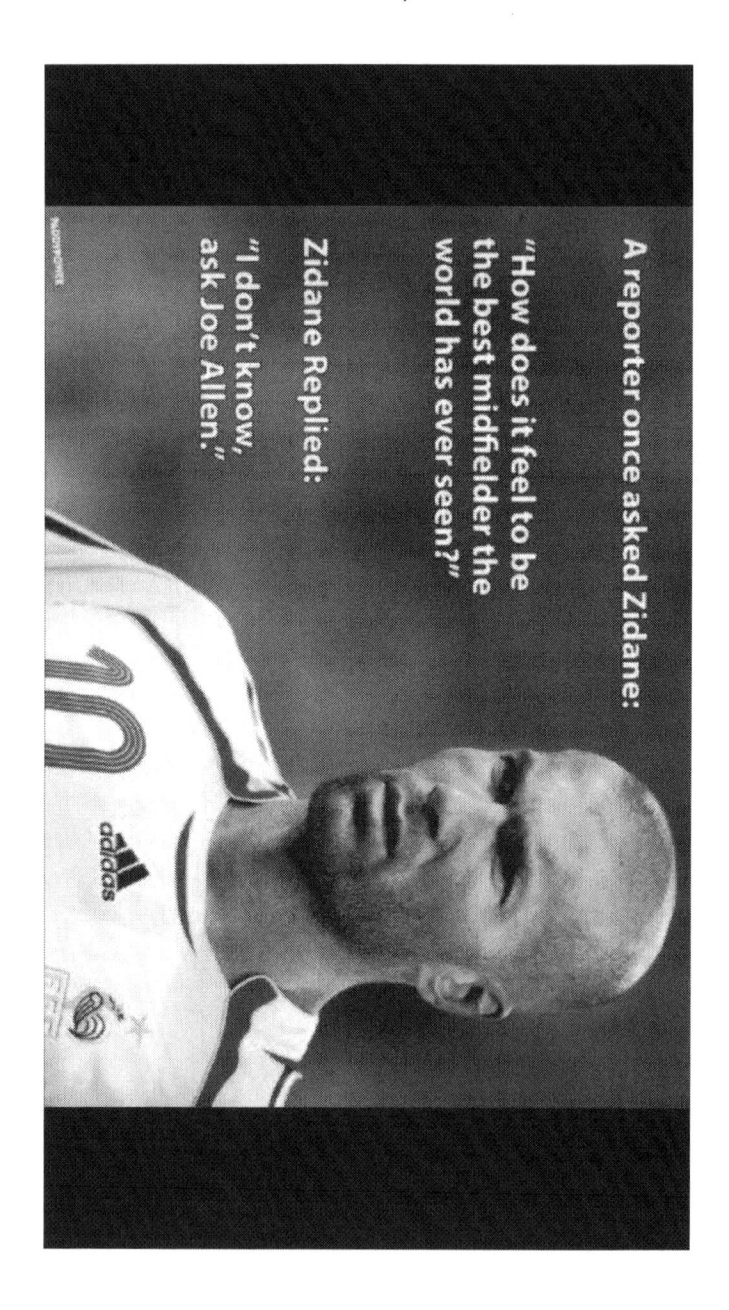

"How does it feel to be the best midfielder the world has ever seen?"

Zidane Replied:

"I don't know, ask Joe Allen."

Please Don't Take Me Home - A Cat Called Robson-Kanu

Andrew Foley Jones 🍴 eating **French cuisine** at 📍 **Restaurant La TUPINA**.
11 June · Bordeaux, France

Beginning to feel the tension; In search of some pre match distraction I found this tray of beautiful radish.

Andrew Foley Jones

Please Don't Take Me Home - A Cat Called Robson-Kanu

Andrew Foley Jones

Jules Jones Peters added 9 new photos — with **Andrew Foley Jones** and **6 others**.
20 June

THERE ARE NO FRONTIERS
That we can't cross tonight
There are no borderlines
To keep us apart... 🖤⚽

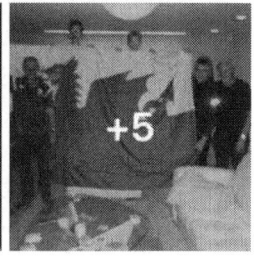

Please Don't Take Me Home - A Cat Called Robson-Kanu

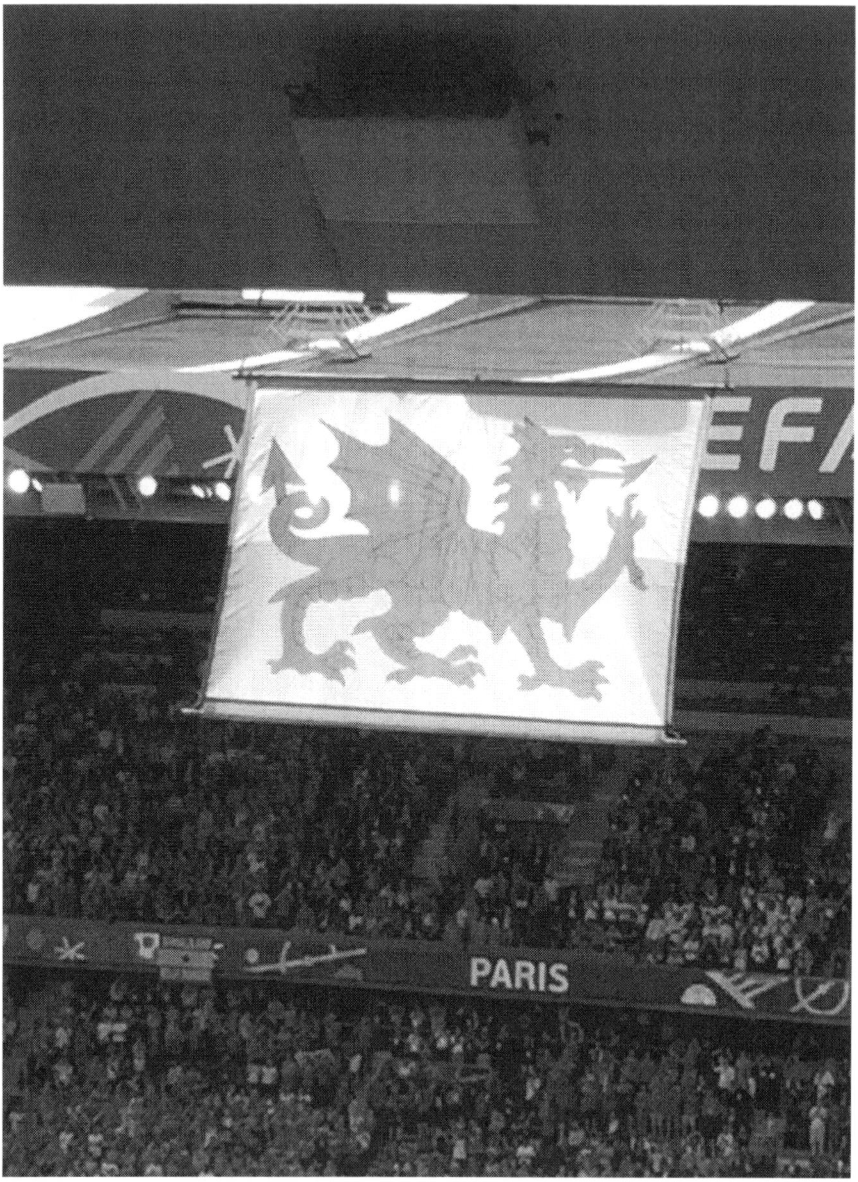
PARIS

Please Don't Take Me Home - A Cat Called Robson-Kanu

•●○○○ vodafone UK 4G   11:36

<   🔍 Sarah Roberts   ⚙

Sarah Roberts shared **Richard Jones**'s post.
10 June

Richard Jones with **Louise Davies-Jones**.
10 June

Some guy called Craig Bellamy with the Macjones massive :-)

👍😃 Ian Davies and 4 others   2 Comments

👍 Like   💬 Comment   ➤ Share

Andrew Foley Jones

Richard Jones with **Andrew Foley Jones** at ♀ **Hilton Vienna Danube Waterfront**.
6 October · Vienna, Austria

We've had worse mornings. Arrived in Vienna and checked into the Hilton across the road from the ground. The entire Welsh team... Continue reading

Please Don't Take Me Home - A Cat Called Robson-Kanu

Only England could manage to exit Europe twice in one week...

Andrew Foley Jones

●●○○○ vodafone UK 4G   11:36

Sarah Roberts

Sarah Roberts shared **Jules Jones Peters**'s post.
11 June

Jules Jones Peters
11 June

C'mon Wales 🖤 Together Stronger

Please Don't Take Me Home - A Cat Called Robson-Kanu

Andrew Foley Jones with **Richard Jones**.
6 July

How much do we not like Ronaldo

Andrew Foley Jones

•●○○○ vodafone UK 4G   11:39

< 🔍 Sarah Roberts   ⚙

Andrew Foley Jones added 18 new photos — 😆 feeling excited at 📍 **Toulouse-purpan** with **Richard Jones**.

21 June · Toulouse, France

Just woke up from this beautiful dream we topped our group in the Euros. Then I found this collection of hats at the base of my bed. This really did happen? After years of sporting disappointment, let's indulge in this moment. And by the way, **Sarah Roberts** please post me out some more lucky underpants.

👍 You, HJ Wilko and 50 others   9 Comments

Please Don't Take Me Home - A Cat Called Robson-Kanu

Sarah Roberts added 3 new photos.
25 June · Duddon

Andrew Foley Jones in total snack heaven

Andrew Foley Jones

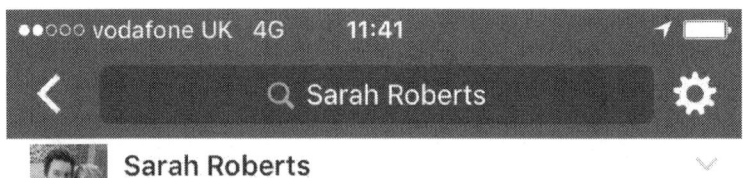

Sarah Roberts
25 June · Picardy, France

Andrew Foley Jones peaked too soon. Crisp coma.

Please Don't Take Me Home - A Cat Called Robson-Kanu

••ooo vodafone UK 4G   11:42

Sarah Roberts

Sarah Roberts added 15 new photos.
26 June · Paris, France

Fantastic trip to Paris with **Andrew Foley Jones Richard Jones** even better now Wales are through to quarter finals. Don't think there is any legal work at Mac Jones being done during June and hopefully early July. 😍✓💋🙈

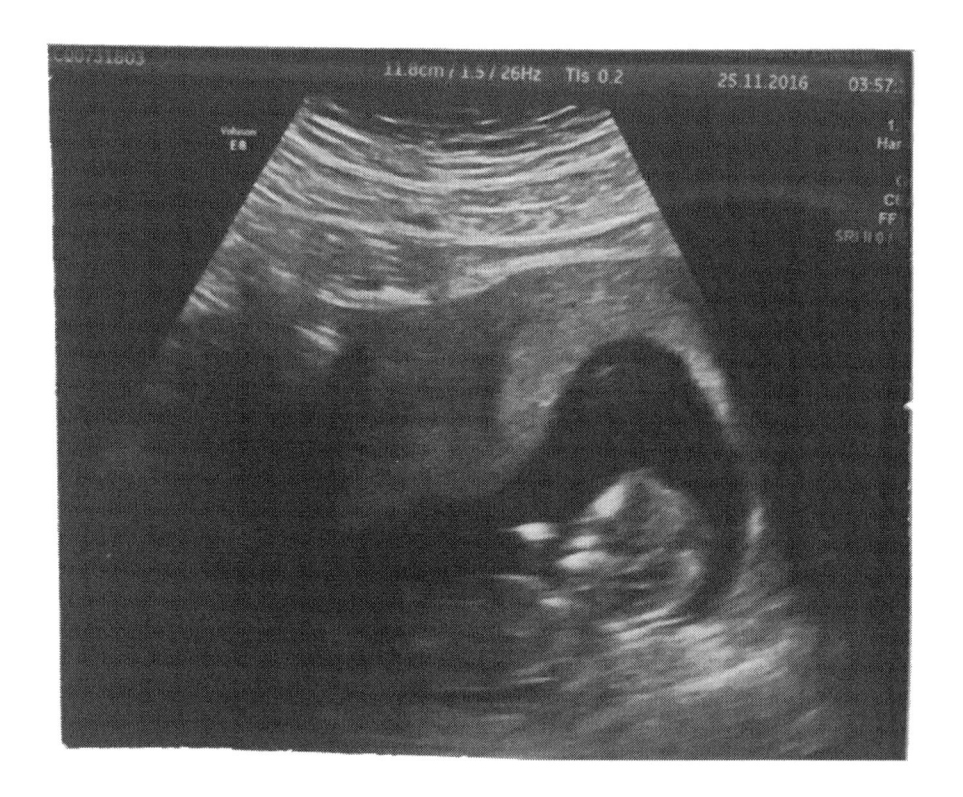

Andrew Foley Jones

Please Don't Take Me Home - A Cat Called Robson-Kanu

Andrew Foley Jones

Printed in Great Britain
by Amazon